CAPTAIN'S BLOG
FOOTBALL, FATHERHOOD AND THE FIGHT FOR PROMOTION

by

Chris Hargreaves

Torbay Books

7 Torquay Road, Paignton, Devon TQ3 3DU

This book simply could not have been written without the help of my wife Fiona, and children, Cam, Issy and Harriet, who I love very much and who have supplied me with endless material.

This applies to the lads at the club as well, obviously apart from the love part.

I must say a big thanks to Andy Phelan, a true gent, Dave Thomas for his guidance and Guy Henderson for his patience.

Also huge thanks to Richard, Damian, Pete, Andy and Tony - without them this season simply would not have happened - and to Jody and John Shelley of Jodes Salon for all their support.

I would also get into big trouble if I did not mention my lovely mum Avy and the big man Martin who, after all, gave me a ball in the first place.

In memory of James Carroll, 1992-2009

Chris Hargreaves, May 2009

First published 2009 Torbay Books
Text copyright Chris Hargreaves

Printed for Torbay Books
7 Torquay Road, Paignton, Devon TQ3 3DU

Front cover photograph by Action Images
Back cover photograph by Casey Levie, courtesy of Torbay News Agency
Cover design by Mike Kowalski
Printed and bound in Great Britain by
CPI Antony Rowe, Chippenham and Eastbourne

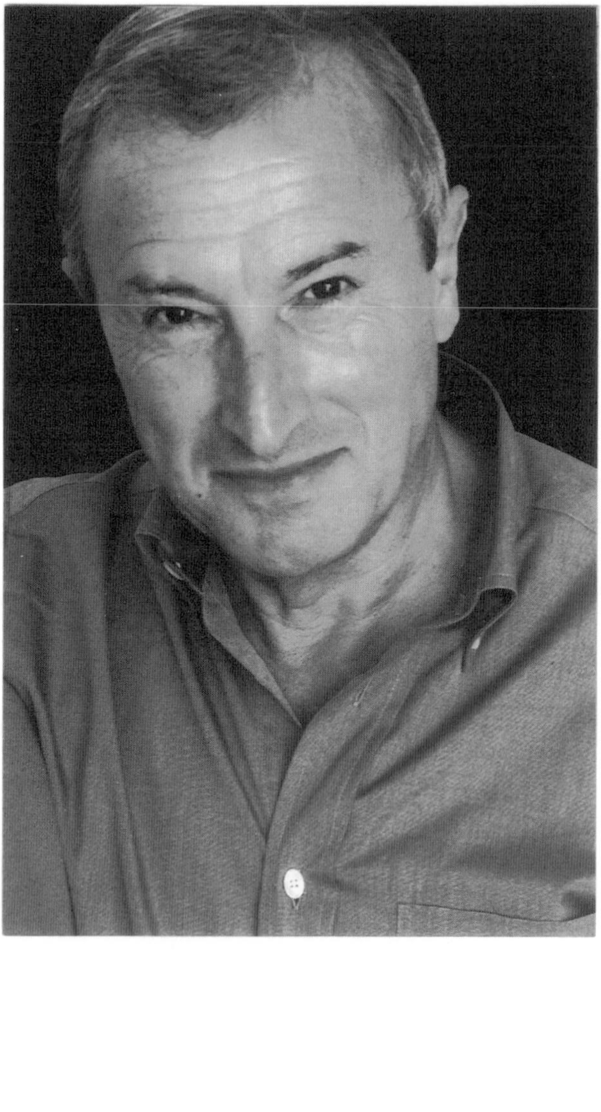

Chris Hargreaves

When Chris Hargreaves scored in the play-off final against Cambridge United it was just about the best goal seen at the new Wembley and a fitting reward for 20 years of unrelenting hard graft.

His glorious moment came just a few days after his 37th birthday and his perfect day ended with Torquay United back in the Football League.

Chris and his family - wife Fiona, the kids Cameron, Isabella and Harriet - had waited a long time for that Wembley triumph. It was the sixth time they'd experienced the agonies of the play-offs.

At Brentford, Oxford, Northampton, Hereford and once at Torquay they'd watched dad's team lose – finally his honesty, commitment and leadership had been rewarded.

Only the Hargreaves family really know how much effort Chris puts into his profession. I'm delighted that he's compiled a book of his Captain's Blogs throughout the season that culminated in that Wembley triumph.

Wembley was Chris's 57th match of the season – that's a tribute to his own personal fitness and dedication. He's already made a mark in the media – but I'd advise him to keep on playing as long as he can. He'll be the first to know when the time has come to stop.

As a lifetime Oxford fan I always admired Chris's approach and appetite for the game. When you want someone in your trench or your team's on the ropes and in need of a warrior and a general – Chris Hargreaves is your man.

I was sorry to see Chris leave Oxford, and it was no surprise that he was 'man of the match' when The Gulls knocked Oxford out of the FA Cup.

I'm so pleased that Chris asked me to write this foreword –his Captain's Blog will be a fascinating read. You can be sure that the author has put heart and soul in it.

Jim Rosenthal, May 2009

Captain's Blog

This is the not-so-secret diary of Chris Hargreaves, 37 years old, father, husband and footballer.

It covers eight months of ups and downs, tears and laughter, and the collapse of Woolworths.

This book will give you an insight into the daily life of 'Tarzan', the captain of Torquay United, a football club desperate for promotion, and a life in Devon of a dad of three crazy kids and a 'non-wag' wife.

The rest, as you will discover, is a mixture of philosophy, anecdotes, anti-inflammatory tablets and ice.

WEDNESDAY, 1 OCTOBER 2008

We have lift-off

OK. So it's the first day of me writing a blog and as much as I would love to sit here with a cup of tea and some decent dunkers typing away for an hour, time is tight. My daughter Issy has been dispatched to gymnastics but my son, Cameron, is at football in 20 minutes. I will have to find him first though – it's the 'can I play out with my mates?' phase. It gets worse – 'The Beast', our affectionately-named two-year-old, is trying to strap her ankle with a bandage (one I brought home from the club) whilst eating an orange, MESSY! Amazingly enough, the strapping isn't for me – it's for my wife, Fiona, who has damaged both ankle ligaments at step aerobics! Showing off trying to impress the teacher, I think! But this has caused me to have to inflict massive culinary pain on the kids by cooking most meals, although last night's bangers and mash was a winner.

Onto football and we have recently had a few days off. I was relieved to get back after having roughly lifted around 200 boxes as well as doing a bit of plumbing, banging, fixing, shouting and even repairing. Yes, house move, and yes, the van we hired broke down... LOVE IT!

This week the lads have had a spring in their step and after a few decent results can look forward to the next month. If training is anything to go by the quality and work-rate from the boys should hold us in good stead, not forgetting the constant banter, topped off this week by Kenny Veysey's home hair dye kit for a fancy dress party. It was SEMI-PERMANENT jet black, so major 'Just For Men' shouts for Ken, who - to be fair - turned up to train this morning with a great false 'tache to match. Good work Ken.

There has also been a run of birthdays at the football club so cakes everywhere, even a homemade special from Mark Ellis, although he would only let the other centre halves have a piece. Don't eat it lads, it's going to give you Delhi belly! Could it be Mark's masterplan to get back in for Saturdays game?

I travelled to see Bristol City versus Plymouth Argyle on Tuesday night and I bumped into Neil 'Razor' Ruddock. He was Bristol City's 'official club photographer' for the night. The highlight for the City fans in the first half was Razor bending down to snap a 'low shot'. In doing so he ripped his tracksuit bottoms right open. To be honest, the pre-match pies were spot on though. I will have to go now, it's a madhouse in here, Harriet (The Beast) is naked outside with a Hoover. Speak soon.

FRIDAY, 3 OCTOBER 2008

The referee's a... well, he's alright actually!

I have seen the light! Although I have already received a few bookings this season - one for dissent and a couple for (five-minute) late challenges - the new respect to referees campaign is having a big effect on me.

This is coming from someone who has received more yellow cards than most, quite a few reds for good measure and a couple of bans for voicing my opinion to refs who I think have cost me promotions and cup victories etc. (no sour grapes here honestly!)

It's either the fact that I have finally chilled out or it's that the refs are more approachable this season but I am even able to call refs by their first name. In our recent game at Wrexham we had the usual meeting in the ref's room. All the officials, both captains and assistant managers were present and the ref said: "Lads, I just want us all to get on and enjoy the game, feel free to call me by my first name or 'Sooty' if you like". I'm thinking 'Sooty? Sooty?' That's unbelievable in the modern game, but great all the same, and true to form I did.

I 'Sooty', 'Sweeped' and 'Sued' him all game, he was a top bloke. No doubt I may lose it again with the officials but I do think times have to change to calm things down on the pitch.

I know, and have had this argument several times with mates who play and support rugby, that the general opinion is 'look at those boys - what an example, total respect for the ref'. Well, to that I say: yes, true - but it's not exactly a great comparison. If one of these boys throws a haymaker in a scrum or stamps on a few legs to get a ball it's a case of 'play on', 'all in the sport, mate' or it's a quick session in the old sin-bin.

Imagine if I threw a quick rabbit punch after a throw-in. I would be at FA HQ sharpish and labelled a football thug.

I'm not saying I want to do that, but in rugby you can take your frustrations out in a tackle or a quick ruck whereas in football the ref is the punchbag verbally. Add to that the fact that there are no instant replays in football - it is tough, but the more approachable a referee is, the better .

It's a hard job being a ref but they sometimes don't help themselves. Remember the ref who infamously booked Gazza after he had dropped his yellow card and was then 'booked' by Gazza himself - a big case of sense-of-humour bypass there.

Anyway let's try to get on with and not surround the ref - as long as he gives us every decision!

Must get off now as my back is beginning to collapse and my left hamstring is burning in a huge way, so its ibuprofen on toast for tea with a side order of crushed ice.

Saturday Night Fever!

Just arrived back home with Cameron after the Stevenage game *(won 3-0)*. Great conditions for football, blowing a gale and raining. But considering the conditions, I thought the lads played well. Three good goals and a solid performance. It must have been a bit nippy in the stands today, so thanks to all who came to support, at least there was something to shout about against a team well-fancied for promotion this season. No one knows how the season will pan out - it seems open for anyone at the moment, so we just need to make sure that we are doing everything in our powers to be one of those teams. This is the only time I will talk about last season and what I will say is we were all devastated with the end result, having to return home with my kids after both play-off semi-final games against Exeter and seeing their faces... it hurt like hell. But it's gone, and it's now onwards and upwards. You can either sit in a corner with your thumb in your mouth or dust yourself off and try again and that's what's gonna happen.

Tonight is going to involve major Saturday night TV, plenty of food and a few glasses of red. Times have changed, it's now a few friends round and all the kids going mental to You've Been Framed, X-Factor and Strictly Come Dancing. In fact, as I speak my kids are on the ceiling in fits of laughter watching a man headbutting a birthday cake and a baby being fired cannon-style over a sofa after over-egging the baby bouncer. Clubbing every weekend may be a thing of the past but me and the wife can still party! The difference now is you pay for it big time the morning after the night before, especially when you have got The Beast demanding to watch Fifi and the Flowertots and wanting a slice of ham at six o'clock in the morning. You just have to dig in and pretend you have had more than three hours' sleep. Tomorrow will involve watching the boy play footy and maybe going to watch the motocross up the road. Cameron and I usually both have bikes but at the moment his is under a pile of stuff in the garage and I have sold mine to avoid doing myself in!

Tommy Northcott

Must not forget to mention the sad news of Tommy Northcott's death. Not only were his football abilities great, 150-odd goals for Torquay, but he was also held in the upmost respect as a person.

Also good luck to Jim Rosenthal, who is running the Great North Run tomorrow in aid of the Sir Bobby Robson Foundation. Sir Bobby is battling cancer again, for the fifth time, but is putting all his efforts in to raise money for cancer charities. I got to know Jim when I was at Oxford and he is a real gent. Blister plasters at the ready mate.

TUESDAY, 7 OCTOBER 2008

Screen test...

Getting ready for the Oxford game this week. It will be good to see some old mates, although in football terms the most I want to be giving any of the lads is a stick of rock after the game. Oxford are another club whose expectations are high but we have to concentrate on ourselves so another good performance is needed. It's another Setanta game and it would be good to continue our recent form in front of the cameras.

Interesting looking at the Premiership at the moment and I reckon the team of the moment has to be Hull - a late run into the play-offs and now 17 points already. An old mate of mine, Dean Windass, fired them into the Premiership in that play-off final, but at the moment he can't get a look-in. Knowing Deano, his presence will still be big both on and off the training ground. When I was playing for Hull, I remember Deano trying to claim a deflected goal after a game he wasn't even playing in!

Back to us and hopefully we will have great support again on Thursday night and more points in the bag.

Gutted

Just got back after the Oxford game - very disappointed, as I'm sure everyone is *(drew 1-1)*. I'm like all the lads and staff - really gutted we didn't win, but I don't want to get into the game, stats, facts, figures, Setanta etc. I just want to get into an ice bath, recover and get ready for the Rushden game, because that is what you have to do. Thanks to all the fans who came tonight. I thought the support was great.

Every little helps...

In a really bad mood today but I am going to try to be consistent and blog win, lose or draw. I did the school run this morning and then returned home to ice my back. It's the last thing you need as a player, getting hit in the ribs after five minutes of the second half of a game you want to do well in, and spending the next 40 struggling and playing badly. A lot of the lads play with knocks etc, the amount of games you play feeling 100 per cent are few and far between. I'm not playing the violin though. I stayed up until about 3am last night thinking about the game. After 20 years it still drives you mad. It's the same for all the players and staff. Taking your work home with you takes on another aspect in football, it's not just very hard to turn off... you don't turn off! Home life is a whole lot better when you're winning and most players, managers and their families I have come across in football feel the same. I thought I would nip into Tesco on the way back and get a few energy drinks, vitamins etc. After filling the old basket with enough stuff to keep a small army awake for a month I spotted a checkout just about empty so I headed for it. TEN minutes later I was still at the same checkout, listening to the troubles of a woman whose bloke had piles talking to the checkout assistant who wasn't happy with her new hair colour. I'm not joking either. I don't know whether they were bothered I was waiting there but they just kept on talking. I stood there, my back on fire, thinking they must be good mates so I kept quiet and dug in. Finally the checkout assistant completed the transaction and said to the woman 'thanks then, nice to meet you'. Need I say more? It finished me off.

Grins and needles...

It's the morning after the Rushden game and the old body is a tad sore. I didn't feel great before the game so Damien Davey, our club physiotherapist, gave me another injection in the back prior to kick-off and a 'booster' at half time. Not very enjoyable, but it had the desired effect - we won and won well *(3-1)*. I thought that there were some great individual performances and collectively we looked strong yesterday. It was great to see so many fans at the game so hopefully as well as getting a suntan, you also returned to Devon having seen a good game. My family stayed in Northamptonshire at the weekend catching up with old friends, enjoying great hospitality and wine (so my wife tells me). It was nice for my children and wife to see an away game. They thought it was funny when after the away fans shouted the obligatory 'where's your caravan', I pointed to the car park. It's harmless banter, especially when you win. Also at the game were my parents, Avy and Martin, who rode down from the east coast to the game on their bike, yes I said bike, 1200cc! I won't tell you how old they are but let's just say they are eligible for cheaper fares. I don't know many miles have been racked up on that bike but I reckon they could give Ewan McGregor and Charlie Boorman a run for their money. If you're reading this A and M, see you soon and lots of love. If you're wondering when I'm going to get political and topical, it's soon. Yes, the credit crunch will be mentioned just as soon as I have opened, and recovered from the shock of, our latest credit card statement.

Tough Love!

I'm taking my children to athletics tonight. They both went down to the local track last week and loved it so it may become a weekly or twice-weekly event. My eldest daughter, Issy, has for the last five-and-a-half years been training and competing in gymnastics. More recently she has been going five nights a week, for three-and-a-half hours each session. For an eight-year-old girl this is a gruelling routine, which she reminds me of constantly when I mentioned my training schedule. The dedication she has shown and the love of doing it has been immense. This constant training has pretty much tired her out though, and has caused a lot of tears in the process, especially recently. So the decision was made for her to take a break, but she still wanted to be active - hence the visit to the local track. Her football-mad brother accompanied her last week and they both really enjoyed it. There was a choice of events including long jump, high jump, javelin, and sprinting. Now instead of five nights a week for Issy, it's two, and for the boy his football-dominated week has a break in it. I don't want to be a pushy dad, I will quite happily settle for a future Olympian and England international. Not forgetting the baby, I reckon she has a great chance of becoming the Devon and Cornwall cream tea-eating champion.

Guru

I was due to be surfing today but have had to cancel due to lack of mobility. Instead I visited Pete Morgan at South Devon College for a bit of manipulation and massage. I'll come back to Pete later. Before I moved down to Devon I hadn't really surfed much, so I was keen to try it. As luck would have it, our pre-season tour was in North Devon so the whole squad piled into the minibus and headed for Westward Ho. The squad was split into three groups. A quick crash course, then it was into the water, and on the day in question the waves were big. Two hours later we all came out battered, bruised and half drowned but with big smiles on our faces and sea tales to tell. Highlights were the manager not seeing Shaun North and surfing through/over him and Kev Nicholson constantly rolling off the board to the amusement of all the lads (sorry mate). A great day though, ending with fish and chips on the sea front and a game of bingo, two fat ladies and a few prizes. Now that's living it up! So the surfing bug was caught. In fact myself, Chris Todd, Lee Hodges and Damo our crack physio even turned round on the way home to catch some more waves (Point Break moment). Since then, I've been surfing a few times and even kayaking with a mate, which was great albeit a bit dodgy on the return journey. My mate's judgment on the water was clouded by Bass beer (quick stop at Turf Locks pub). I also did a bit of jet-skiing on Exmouth seafront a few weeks ago, my brother and a mate brought a 1500cc supercharged machine to town. I think they were determined to kill me on this channel-crossing monster. I took it a bit steadier on my own, well for the first five minutes anyway. We are now a full-on surfing/skiing family. Even The Beast dons a wetsuit and eats waves. Literally.

Finally back to Pete Morgan, the Guru. Pete lectures at South Devon College and has set up his own physiotherapy business. He also comes to games and visits after training to help out Damien and give his expert opinion. He is one funny man, his stories are legendary, including sledging with his dogs (being dragged for two miles - the sledge broke!) and sneezing egg mayonnaise on a date (there was no second date!) Must not forget to mention his devilish good looks, if you're reading this Pete I'll e-mail you my address and you can send me the cheque in the post!

THURSDAY, 16 OCTOBER 2008

Busy day...

Mini-blog as it's a busy day today. Just returned home from training, the children are back from school so it's a quick feed time/homework session.

Cam is at football for 6pm and Issy is at athletics for 6.30pm so it's a 9pm return to the house to face a very tense wife (Harriet, The Beast, is a menace at the moment). Then there's the problem of getting the kids to bed before their parents. Looking forward to a nice anti-inflammatory sandwich for supper. Well done England, and look on the bright side Guy Ritchie - you'll be in for around £50million (pre-nup permitting).

Junk food

Just arrived at the hotel after another mammoth journey north. Tonight's evening meal was another Friday night classic - in fact it was probably the 1,000th dry, basic pasta dish I have consumed in my career, a sand-based sauce with a very fed-up chicken. The whole squad usually eats together, then it's back to our rooms to relax. We are paired off as 'roomies' at the start of the season and barring injury and illness this usually lasts the duration. This means you have to choose wisely or you could be in for one long season. Benyon, Ellis and Rice are just a few examples of the dangers out there. With my usual room-mate, Chris Todd, facing an operation, I have had the luxury of my own room for a month, which after the usual week of madness at home comes in handy. Most of the lads fill their bags with snacks, some healthy, some not. The younger lads can get away with the 'seefood' diet of anything goes. In fact I have just returned from the Rowe/Thompson room and witnessed a sight that would give Gillian McKeith a heart attack. Still, it doesn't do those lads any harm - they could give Usain Bolt a few endurance sessions. Myself and Steve Woods may read the papers in the bar and have a moan about something, e.g. the price of the weekly shop (it's an age thing) and then it's off to hit the sack - which I now intend to do. Looking forward to the game, hoping to keep our form and run going.

Apology

Firstly apologies about the lack of blog yesterday. It was a very late return to Devon last night after the Ebbsfleet game. The game went according to plan *(won 2-0)*, again great individual performances and together the team looked and felt strong. It was good to beat a team that we have performed badly against in the past. We started similarly to last season's FA Trophy final against them, but this time we took our chances and never looked in danger. We now have a break from the league so it was an important three points gained, enabling us to look forward to the cup knowing that we are in a good position in the table –a position that we must try to build on in every game. The team always appreciate the support home and away, it's again good to know the journey back for the fans and ourselves is much sweeter after a victory.

It was sad to see the news about Wakefield Rugby League prop Adam Watene, who collapsed and died during a routine weights session last Monday. At 31 and in his prime, it must be a traumatic time for his fellow players, family and friends. I think it's quite poignant that in the same week there has been the well-documented death of Dan James, a former England Students rugby player. Eighteen months ago during a training session with Nuneaton he suffered a terrible injury resulting in paralysis from the neck down. Since then he had constantly expressed his wish to die, saying he didn't feel it was a life worth living. Together with his parents he travelled to the Swiss euthanasia clinic, Dignitas, where his wish was granted. I'm sure if you're reading this you may be thinking 'wow, lighten up mate'. But I just thought about Bill Shankly's famous quote about football being more important than life and death. As much I and many other players would run through the proverbial brick wall for our sport... no, not in football, rugby or any other sport is it more important than life and death.

OK, so it's 7.30pm, Cam has just told me he has a project to finish for school tomorrow, Issy is creating a beauty spa in her room and the baby is dive bombing off our bed. Add that to the fact I have just treated myself to a massive stub on the toe, it's time to go.

On the buses

Following on from the small mention in the last blog about return journeys being better after victories, I thought I would give you a small insight into what goes on on the team coach. On the coach, you will find the back row boys, the driver's mate, the networkers and the old-schoolers. Tim Sills and Kev Nicholson sit at the back, fine-tuning their pub quiz knowledge or watching a DVD together. It's a cross between Film 2008 and The Weakest Link. In front of this, you will find Robbo, silent but deadly. I forgot to mention Elliot Benyon, who is usually found skulking about, right in the corner at the back. He could be making a den or collecting and torturing small insects. Then further on are the two tables where the old-schoolers sit - Mansell, Woods, Hodges, Adams, Todd, Brough and Hargeaves. It's a hierarchy thing, it takes years to get in these Mafioso seats. Card schools, games and hardcore banter are found here, so sit in at your peril. Next in line you will find the networkers – D'Sane, Stevens, Thompson, Carayol, Green and Poke. They will be talking to each other and to their mates on their phones, laptops, iPhones, blackberries and blueberries in 'txt spk': m8, gr8, innit, winit, phat, fin and other mad abbs (abbreviations). The next in line is Nicky Wroe, who is ready to step up to the old-schoolers but is not yet ready to leave the networkers. He also may not want to leave his position in front of one of the TVs. The TV doesn't work but we all live in hope. Opposite Nicky is Scott Bevan, our new keeper and at 6ft 6in he loves the easyjet legroom and the breezeblock seats. Then it's management and directors: The Manager, Northy, Ken, Damo and Brian Palk, a club director who without fail is the first to buy the drinks after games, cheers Bri. Matches are watched here, positions decided etc. It's a good place to be but expect a fierce text from one of the lads if you sit here as a player. I get a lot of texts! At the front you will find the driver's mate, Mark Ellis. They share the same interests, namely sitting at the front and not talking. To be fair to Mark though, he has been playing Championship Manager for the last 18 months. It must be for charity. Also at the front is Wayne Carlisle, who likes it there simple as that so it is! Roaming down the aisle you may find Martin Rice, who can't sit still, or one of the young apprentices, often Raiff, thinking about where to sit for the best. Finally you will find our traffic-finding driver, Dave. I'm sure he does it on purpose but the onboard temperature is constantly turned up to volcanic. By the end of most trips you will find the lads down to their boxers and rare tropical plants growing at the back, the heat is that intense. Add that to the fact he always finds a better route via a road he has spotted, like the B11115555566662, and you can imagine the insults that fly down to the front of the bus. We love you really Dave. So that's it other than to say they are a really great bunch of people who win lose and draw together.

TUESDAY, 21 OCTOBER 2008

Babyccino

Day off today and with my wife out on an interview, I was left with the whirlwind, our two-year-old baby daughter Harriet. So instead of going to the local spit and sawdust gym for a big weights session, me and 'H' are face-to-face and there was only ever going to be one winner. You would think that the morning would consist of her wrecking the house, then maybe us feeding the ducks, but no: it's 2008 and the modern baby has changed dramatically. First it was 'choo-choo daddy'. Fair enough, but it wasn't playing with a train set, it was actually on a real train. Off to the station we went with 'H' walking the first 100 yards then sitting on my shoulders for the next two miles. Why the train, and where to? I asked Harriet this question and the answer was a sort of 'come on Dad, get with it... 'go for a Cappuccino'. Yep, it's started. Unbelievable I know, we are sat down in a Costa Coffee house with a Cappuccino for one and a Babyccino for Harriett (frothy milk with chocolate sprinkles). It's going to be a testing few years with now three shopaholics in the family. It's just a good job I've got the boy for back-up.

It's a marathon...

Things are hotting up in the Blue Square Premier League and we are in there fighting. It is a good position we find ourselves in now after a shaky start to the season, although a few of the early results could have swung our way. The day-to-day training is sharp and all the players are focused on the same objective of winning games. Like all seasons, there will be ups and downs but at the moment there is a really good feeling in the squad. It's also a great sign at a club to see players who aren't in the team for whatever reason still training hard and being fully behind the rest of the lads. We look forward to the cup games but as always the aim is promotion. Very tired today as I've been coaching tonight, just had my tea at 9.30pm. The last mention goes to Grandma's arrival. The children are excited (treats and hugs!), my wife is excited (breaks from the madhouse!) and I'm excited (full-on dinners!). Grandma's journey was from Lincolnshire and the journey time? TEN HOURS, yes 10 joyous hours on Britain's road network and the culprit not a car, not a bike, but a National Express coach. This still seems a marathon journey, even on a coach. I'm just wondering if Dave, our team coach driver, was behind the wheel...

Ace

Can't believe I forgot to mention Lee 'Lambster' Mansell. He is considering doing some voluntary work for the RSPCA after his recent impressive rescue of a wild animal. There was a movement at the bottom of the garden one morning so Lee shot down to discover a friendly but very thin badger. After phoning some of his teammates and the RSPCA, he waited with the poor starving animal to receive the praise of his mates and of the rescue team. They all arrived together, and yes it was an animal, yes it was friendly... but badger it was not. Freddie the ferret had escaped from a nearby house. It was an easy mistake to make. After all, badgers are very shy, quite big and are only seen at night, so good effort 'Lambster', but Ace Ventura Pet Detective can rest easy.

X and Y

Even with a gale blowing across the racecourse, training was again very good today. The gym was busy after training as the lads continue their strength/beach body workouts. I have been known to do the odd weight session, but the front runner in that department at the moment has to be our new goalkeeper, Scotty Bevan. With him not being able to train fully today he started pumping iron instead about 9.30am. Unbelievably, as we returned to the gym to stretch and start our own weight sessions, the big man was still at it. That's a three hour-plus beasting. I know he's having a barren spell at the moment in the dating arena but that's a lot of pent-up anger. Just for you Scott, I'm going to list your qualities and interests. There's the Chris Martin (of Coldplay) likeness, the love of weights, the love of food, the love of tattoos, not forgetting the tallness and the love of diving about in the mud. So in a nutshell, if you're a 6ft 4in mud-wrestling, tattooed, Coldplay fan, please leave your details and I'll make sure Scott gets them.

FRIDAY, 24 OCTOBER 2008

Cup fever from Torquay to Milan

Great days! The FA cup is upon us, brilliant moments and memories from years past. That's what this competition is all about, so let's hope we have a good run this season and put a smile on the chairman's face. I saw a friend of mine today, Richard Carr-Hyde, a brilliant chiropractor based in Newton Abbot. He was telling me about his recent trips to AC Milan on a consultancy basis to work alongside his friend, the head of the medical department Jean Pierre Meersseman. Jean Pierre probably lives near Lake Como in a mountainside palace with butler service and enough horsepower in the drive to impress even Jeremy Clarkson. On his most recent trip, Rich was working with Filipo Inzaghi, an Italian international and Milan star. 'OK, enough', I'm saying to Rich, but no - there's more. All players at Milan have a 10-point checklist before going into a game, psychological analysis, blood tests, vitamin and mineral levels, and levels of CO_2 expelled are just some of the tests undertaken. That's before we get to any 'niggle' a player might have. If a player fails to score above 6.8 he doesn't even play. This 10-point system has been effective in that the injury rates have been reduced by about 96 per cent. Since Meersseman has been at Milan, the squad has been dramatically reduced, no doubt saving tens of millions. Not bad for someone who was already very successful in his own practice, but if Silvio Berlusconi were to offer you a couple of million a year at an Italian giant... hey, why not? I'm just wondering whether a tight groin, a glass ankle and having to have a couple of injections in the ribs will keep me out of the game tomorrow. Oh, and then there's my mental state, which after hearing all this is quite fragile. Hey, it's the FA Cup though, 10-point test or not. A great insight to life at a big club there. It's also going to be Meersseman's final decision on whether David Beckham passes his medical, no pressure there then. I know after speaking to a few Italian players over the years how dedicated they are and I'm not sure how managers and chairman in Italy would handle Joey Barton. I don't buy into the second, third and fourth chances, we all know if he was in the lower leagues and not worth £6million he would be dropped like a stone, a long, long way. Rant over, speak soon.

Job done

Potential banana skin over with *(beat Chipstead 4-1)*. Thanks for your
support today on a very cold afternoon. Although the performance was not
great, the scoreline looks decent and we have progressed to the first round
proper. These cup games are vital to the club on the financial side and we
hope to do well this season in the cup competitions. I spoke to Alex Rowe,
our chairman, after the game and he was relieved to be through. Clubs in
the lower leagues have to be run with great care otherwise there can be real
problems. If it wasn't for people like Alex and other local
businessman/directors who love the club and are prepared to outlay the
money, I'm sure it would be a different story. All clubs lose money - even
Man Utd are a bit overdrawn, about £700million at the last count. A cup
run for a big club is just as important, albeit on a different scale. If Leeds
United had got into the Champions League a few years back they might still
be in the Premiership and would not be continuing to pay some player's 40
grand-a-week wages, even after they have left the club. While I'm on the
subject of support, my sponsor Jody Shelley (from Jodes Salon) is another
person who gives up a lot of time and money to support the club. She also
does a wicked makeover. My wife has been on the receiving end of a few. I
may delete that or say it was a typing error. If anyone is going to finally
chop my locks it will be Jodie. I've been tempted many times, and by
around 2020 I will be ready for the cull, but for now a short back and sides
for me will still consist of 4mm off the ends. Final mention is to Albert, a
Grimsby Town fan and ex-resident who is currently living in Oxford. He
popped into the changing room before our recent game with Oxford to say
hello and he handed me another gift. Albert has given me a few gifts
including a big bottle of whisky, five packs of cards, some old coins, and the
latest gift - a small hip flask and miniature of whisky. Albert obviously
wants me to become a hard drinking gambler, but what a great character. If
you can fathom the computer Albert, my Dad says he will put the kettle on
for the next time you visit home and pop into 'Martin Hargreaves

Motorcycles'. I will send the whisky up for you to top up your tea with. Cheers to The Ancient Mariner.

Morning TV

This is an early posting on the blog today due to a couple of reasons, namely the clocks going back and the baby waking up, but also the fact that we are having a day out. Yes, it was my turn to rise with Harriet this morning and, deep joy, it was 5.50am. I tried to persuade Hatty that it was still night-time but it was in vain, soon we were both downstairs watching Teletubbies and reading Flora's Blanket. Why is it always the same? If I had gone to bed at 10pm last night, 'H' would have been in bed till 9am this morning.

It's my fault, I know, but when everybody had gone to bed, my mind was still in the Red Bull zone. I stayed up and trawled through the offerings on late night/early morning TV. First I caught the second half of the Bundesliga game between Bayern Munich and Cologne, a great game ending 4-2 to Bayern. While this was on I kept flicking over to watch the 100 Greatest Scary Moments. In the end the final three arrived.

In 3rd place, Jaws. Bit of a surprise there, especially when Spielberg explained that the mechanical fake shark broke down so they had to drag it along. Scary eh! At number 2 was The Exorcist. A real heart-warmer this one, a young girl is possessed by the devil complete with white eyes and a deep voice. The winner, not my favourite, was The Shining, the big scene involving Jack Nicholson battering a door down with an axe for five minutes. When he finally popped his head through the smashed door, to the delight of the screaming girl, he actually made up the next line. 'Heeeeeeeeere's Johnny' used to be the catchphrase on the Johnny Carson show. Statto! I also got a late-night text from a mate with an invitation to his birthday meal. Michael 'Slipmat' or 'Chatty' Chapman is going to be 40, oh dear the big one. I'm sure when it's mine (in 10 yrs...) I'll be worried as well. Chatty was my next-door-neighbour when I played for Hull City and we had some great laughs. I once wallpapered the whole outside of his house. It took me all day but it was worth it. Why? Well, to cut a long story short, I found out that he and another mate had broken into my house after a night out while I was sleeping had made themselves a pile of cheese toasties, too much evidence left at the scene lads! It's just a good job I didn't wake up and go downstairs prepared to greet the burglars and start windmilling. I also sabotaged a tennis date Chatty had with a young lady by hiding in the bushes and making constant animal noises. He said to his date it was a squirrel nest, but his game went to pot - especially after the elephant noise in the second set. Add that to the fact he nearly killed us on a railway track when he was throwing a few shapes to some music whilst driving his battered VW Scirocco, I think there could be fireworks when we reunite. See you at the York game 'Slipmat', tight shirt and fairy bun ban in place.

MONDAY, 27 OCTOBER 2008

Factoid...

It was great to see Chris Todd at the game on Saturday. Toddy had an operation on Tuesday to repair a tear in his stomach, the resulting scars are impressive. Hopefully the rehab will go well and we will see him in action again soon. He explained to me that it is very painful when he laughs so I recommended a short stay with our driver, Dave. That should do the job. Another player in the wars is Chris Robertson, who damaged ankle ligaments last week. It's incredible how often you are injured after, not during, training. That's exactly what happened on this occasion. Robbo, myself and Kev Nicholson had set up a few cones to do some sprint work and within five minutes Robbo had turned his ankle. Unfortunately this means a fair few weeks out for the big fella, so again fingers crossed it's a speedy recovery. I'm sure he will want to return quickly, he has been playing really well. His pockets are also that deep, I'm talking ankle depth, that his lack of appearance money will be driving him mad.

STOP PRESS! The blog has been criticised, and this is from friends of mine. No, it is not the punctuation or the grammar, as you may think - but apologies for both. It is, in fact, the lack of facts. I'm full of bizarre information and useless facts and I haven't included any. Get your pen and paper and a cup of tea and I will begin.

Every day we drink 165 million cups of tea, importing 150 tonnes a year. Forty million burgers are sold every day by McDonalds. A lightning bolt is five times hotter than the sun, golfers beware. The sun is 330,330 times bigger than the earth. A square piece of paper cannot be folded in half more than seven times (I know you'll try that one). There are no clocks in Las Vegas casinos (I wonder why). There are 194 countries in the world, the smallest being The Vatican City, (it's in Rome). A cockroach can still survive if it loses its head but only for about two weeks as it eventually dies of starvation. The state of Florida is larger than England. Tom Jones' real name is Thomas Woodward and Courtney Love's is Michelle Harrison. The Amazon rain forest gives us 20 per cent of the world's oxygen, contains a quarter of the world's species and takes in one fifth of the worlds CO_2. There are 1.2 billion people living in poverty worldwide despite the fact that there are about 10 million millionaires. And if you think that the 'war on terror' has gone quiet, it hasn't. America is still spending $100million a day fighting the Taliban, while just $7million is spent on the 11 million Afghans in need of aid. Staying in Afghanistan, during recent ferocious fighting with the Taliban, Cpl Paul Knapp said: "In 18 minutes of solid fighting we dropped 176 mortar bombs and fired 9,000 rounds."

I know what you're saying: 'Statto', 'Bore off' etc etc. Sticks and stones will not break my bones (we're not in Roman times) and words will never hurt me, I have heard them all before: 'Gyppo', 'where's your caravan', and 'you're past it' are just a few. And that's just from my family.

Four seasons in one day...

Freezing cold, then quite warm, raining heavily, then really cold. That sums up this morning's weather at the racecourse. It's pretty isolated out there so we get a full range of the elements, but not usually in a 15-minute spell. Environmentalists would save a lot of time and money monitoring climate change if they just spent a morning at the racecourse. After training had finished and we'd braved 'Hurricane Newton Abbot', the reigning head tennis champions Woods and Hargreaves took on more contenders. Nicholson and Sills stepped up to challenge the throne. Overhead kicks, aces, diving headers... it had everything. But after 40 minutes and more dodgy line calls than John McEnroe ever received it was over. All-comers welcome on Thursday again, the old boys remain unbeaten.

The summer that never was is over. Yes, the clocks have gone back an hour - meaning it is now dark at 4.30pm. Introduced in 1916, it was primarily as an energy-saving measure in wartime. Without the change, children - especially in Scotland - would be going to school all year in the dark, meaning extra lighting and power would be needed. History lesson over. It is now dark early afternoon, which is not good. The only bonus is that Halloween is on Friday. As of 4 o'clock, the Hargreaves household will turn into the haunted house, complete with scary music in the background, a witch roaming the corridors (my wife dresses up) and the children dragging me round the village until their sweet bags are at breaking point. It should be fun.

Finally I must thank friends of ours who invited us over for a dinner party last night. Homemade samosas to start, homemade curry to follow and even homemade soufflé for dessert. Great food and a good laugh, all in all it was a quality night topped off with the most amazing family photos...

Credit Crunch? What Credit Crunch?

Could my regular Friday night TV be under threat? It usually involves Jonathan Ross interviewing guests and friends, but this time I think he may have got himself into a bit of bother. I enjoy watching the show on Fridays as JR does his stuff. He has great guests (the recent visit of Stevie Wonder was brilliant) and great banter. Initially after hearing he and Russell Brand had been suspended I thought 'over-reaction - get a grip, whoever has complained' (10,000 people phoned the BBC about the radio show they were presenting together). I have since heard the phone call made to Andrew Sachs (Manuel in Fawlty Towers) and the answerphone message left was... let's say controversial. Since then, both have been suspended and I bet they are sweating buckets while on gardening leave awaiting their punishment. I would be really surprised if the BBC axed two of its biggest stars, especially Jonathan Ross who has millions of viewers and is on millions of pounds. A slap on the wrists maybe. The lesson must be to avoid Russell Brand and live radio at all costs. Still on the Fawlty Towers theme, and the hotel that Michael Poke (our currently injured on-loan keeper) has been staying in this season is The Gleneagles, the original Fawlty Towers. Lots of pictures and memorabilia but no Basil, Sybil or in fact Manuel, and the food has definitely improved over the years.

Christmas is upon us and judging by the queues in most shopping centres the credit crunch is on the back burner. You have to keep your elbows in position like a marathon runner when shopping otherwise prepare to be trodden on and left with the piles of clothes strewn over most shop floors. I managed one hour today with the girls until alarm bells started ringing in my back and stomach. The only thing I can bear to buy on these dangerous assault course visits is food and coffee so for me it will be the normal annual Christmas Eve mercy mission.

Two thank-yous today. Firstly Mel at South Devon College, who broke me - in a good way though (massage) - and secondly Dan next door, who I have just seen return to the house with surfboards on the roof rack. Thanks for the invite mate.

Pop Idol

The music industry has seen the likes of Will Young, Shane Ward, Leona Lewis and even Paul Potts shoot to stardom through talent shows. Now there is a new kid on the block, and who is he? Tim Sills! After taking victory in last season's karaoke, he went home with the 'mike'. Sillsy gained a belief that he too could be the new singing sensation. OK, there's the build-up, now for the facts. After sending in a demo, Tim was accepted to the auditions for 'Don't Forget the Lyrics', the Sky One show hosted by Shane Ritchie. Members of the public are invited to win up to £250,000 by simply remembering the lyrics to some of the best-known songs ever written. At the audition, Tim had to sing a song of his choice. Then he was asked to speak about himself for a couple of minutes. He could have blown it here as there was a time limit. There's only so long you can talk about last season's overhead kick, great goal though it was. The song went well - Tim said he belted out a great rendition of Wham's Club Tropicana. Then for the charm offensive and then the wait. And yes, I can report that out of thousands of applicants, our Tim is down to the last 60. He is literally a cat's whisker away from appearing on the show. This is the format - each contestant is given nine categories, behind each is two songs. They pick a song and sing along with the band reading the lyrics from a screen. When the band stops and the words disappear you have to carry on filling in the lyrics. The first song is worth £500, the second £1,000, the third £2,500 and if you get the fourth, you win a guaranteed £5,000. Remember five more, Timmy baby, and you are picking up a cool £250,000 – and, who knows, maybe a visit from Simon Cowell. So sometime soon you may recognise one of the contestants and lots of the audience (Dave, start the coach!) on 'Don't Forget The Lyrics'.

Monster mash

With Crawley slipping up last night we have a great opportunity to put more pressure on the clubs around us. There are no easy games in the Conference any more and Mansfield's visit to Plainmoor will be no different. We will be doing our best to keep the run going. This may read like the standard pre-match hype, but it's the mindset you have to have as a player, coach or manager. We all leave the club on a Friday and try to relax in the 24 hours prior to the game, but at the back of your mind you know that the time is nearing to switch on and go to work. In saying that, it's quite hard to relax when you have got a devil, two witches, a vampire and a skeleton walking around the house. Our home is fully kitted out in Halloween attire and open to trick or treaters. It will be the same story at most of the homes of players at TUFC, especially those that have children. In fact, Stevie Adams, our midfield dynamo, will be revelling in tonight's Halloween fun. Nicknamed 'The Ghoul' (a likeness in colour), I'm sure Stevie will be very convincing when opening his door to visitors. Whether or not they stay long enough to grab a few sweets is another story.
I think Stevie thought he had turned the corner when he joined Torquay, but the nickname we gave him brought him back down to earth with a bang. Unknown to us Stevie, was called 'The Ghost' at Plymouth Argyle, how's your luck?

A big weekend of sport awaits with Lewis Hamilton in Brazil aiming to become a world champion and England's cricketers in Antigua aiming to become very rich. Good luck to both. Must go, I think Stevie is at the door...

Turmoil

Another good result today *(beat Mansfield Town at home, 2-0)*. Conditions were not great but after seeing out the first half against the wind we felt that we could push on in the second half and that's exactly what happened. Again thanks to all who came to support us this afternoon in extremely cold conditions. I'm sure you were all relieved to be getting in your houses and cars and thawing out. It's a short blog today as my stomach is in turmoil, maybe due to the happy pills I have consumed. Our weekly huddle to announce any special news took place as usual. The announcement was a good one. Kevin Nicholson, my shower-loving team-mate, finally got down on one knee and asked/begged the lovely Jenny to be his wife. After a long delay (remember the strawberries Jen) the answer was a yes. This follows the news that Kev and Jen are expecting their first child. So lots to look forward to, including sleepless nights, no spare time, no money and - the worldwide favourite - the 'headache'. Only joking, great times ahead. I can honestly say they are two of the nicest people you will ever come across, love you both to bits so huge congrats. I will share some of the laughs Kev and myself had while 'lodging' together last year soon, but for now adieu.

SUNDAY, 2 NOVEMBER 2008

Apology

The apology is regarding the Rushden game blog. I happened to mention that my parents were eligible for cheaper fares. It was a misprint. It was supposed to say cheaper shares. They are both keen stock market followers, my mistake. My lovely mum, Averil (have I mentioned the ex-beauty queen title?) is often having to dress down so not to upstage her friends, and without bias is beautiful, funny and intelligent. My dad is my dad. You know, usual father and son stuff - 'don't mess with me or I'll break you, son'. A great man, end of story. I hope that has been cleared up. Love always, see you both soon.

P.S Keep up the good work Mark (my brother), it will be worth it mate.

Onto football and we have a break from the league in order to play two cup games in two different competitions. Firstly we play Weymouth tomorrow night in what I'm sure will be another hard game. Not too far to travel though, which is good for us players and for our fans. Then we face Evesham on Saturday, who I'm sure will be coming into town hoping for an upset. These two games will be approached the same as any league game, we aim to keep our run going.

Winner / Coffee time

Winner!!!
THE HARGREAVES HOUSEHOLD HAS JUST GONE CRAZY. It was lost then it was won, a last-lap victory for Lewis Hamilton. Sport at its best. Even Harriet, our two-year-old baby was jumping up and down, shouting 'Come on Hammy, come on Hammy'. Massa was in tears, his team thought he'd won it, but no - it was Lewis at the death who took a great victory.

As mentioned in the last blog I have a few stories to tell about the time myself and my team-mate Kevin Nicholson spent lodging together last season. We had both just signed for Torquay, my family were still in Northamptonshire and Kev's girlfriend was in Derby. Initially we both joined Chris Robertson at a local hotel, but after a few weeks we decided to move into Chris Todd's house. He was about to move out so it worked very well. Or so we thought. The hotel was fine to begin with but after a month of eating out and seeing the same four walls of your room the decision was made. Add to that the fact that Kev was still in his 'dungeon room' and my suite was roomy but minus five degrees at night, it was time to go. I think Robbo stayed because he had negotiated a washing-up rota in the kitchen. Chris Todd's house was just what we needed - a base while we both house-hunted, and a bit of extra space, as well as a cooker. I had been used to full-on days in Northants, what with the commute to Brentford and then Oxford, as well as a soccer school and a new baby. My wife also worked full time, so moving to this house and kicking back was bliss. I mean bliss while missing everyone, obviously. So mine and Kev's days together began - training first, followed by our daily trip to the shop where the big decisions were made - what was for tea, and could Kev force himself to have a pudding? Back at the house it would be a quick game of pre-dinner darts, and then the main event. Gordon Ramsay, eat your heart out. The food produced was top drawer, although I thought you overdid the pasta a few times, Kev. Then the games began. I'm not talking PlayStation here, not my era - too old. I'm talking psychological games. I learnt in the early weeks all about Kev's loves and hates. The huge love of showering three or four times a day, the love of shutting doors and turning all lights off, the love but denial of chocolate, and the love of answering the phone. And the hates: not showering three or four times a day, me driving with my knees, me leaving the lights on, me not shutting doors, me eating chocolate, me walking about naked, me swearing, me not answering my phone and anyone wearing dangly jewellery. No, you can't explain that one. A special week for me began with a visit from Jenny, and while Kev was upstairs setting up his two-hourly shower routine, I searched out the cold water stopcock under the sink. With Jen's permission, it was turned off and the nightmare started. Kev would shout down that the shower was melting him while we giggled away like schoolkids. I would turn the tap on and off for a few minutes then leave it off. He would usually have to run a bath and wait an hour and a half for it to cool down. It would still be red hot though - Kev would return sweating, not good for someone who is shower-dependant. I would then sneak it back on and shoot upstairs, shouting down 'you're not going to believe it mate, it's fine now'. There were even a few nights that Kev would have to go to bed 'dirty'. I kept this going for a week but in the end it was breaking him, so I stopped - only telling him when we both moved out.

We had the darts, the fine food, the shopping trips, the TV nights, but then came a bombshell. One afternoon, Kev said 'shall we go for a coffee?' Now we already looked like a couple, but for me, a northern monkey and non-coffee drinker, this suggestion was big. But I did it and I have to say it was

33

good. A cup of coffee, maybe a cake and a read of the papers, relaxing was the way forward. We had the odd strange glance but otherwise it was spot on. It had to come to an end though, especially when Chris Todd took the TV and turned the heating off. Our spouses had also made the move to Devon but we definitely learnt a lot from each other during those times. I learnt that you don't have to swear constantly, that you can answer the phone, that doors and lights can be shut and turned off and that being fully clothed is also good. I am now a better driver and a coffee drinker.

And for Kev? Well, he can be found driving about naked and swearing in the middle of the day while leaving all the lights and doors on and open at home. So it has to be said we both benefited from the experience. Great days though. Cheers Kev.

WEDNESDAY, 5 NOVEMBER 2008

Christmas Lists

It's 12.15 am. I have just returned from the game against Weymouth *(won 3-0)*, it's all quiet here so I thought I would take the opportunity to type away. The game went well, a very professional display, a clean sheet, three good goals, job done. Now on to the next game. Again thanks for the support tonight, on a weekday and with work tomorrow it's obviously a big ask so we all really appreciate that.

I was a bit reflective last night, the children had decided to write and post their Christmas lists to Santa. As they were busily writing away I was watching the news, the crisis in Congo was on, basically tens of thousands of refugees needing water, food and clothing. Some families there hadn't eaten for a week. I thought to myself that I start having hot sweats if I haven't eaten for a few hours, never mind a day or a week. Then there's the annual pilgrimage everyone makes to the supermarket to load the old trolley up for Christmas. A bizarre rumour usually starts somewhere that all shop workers are striking for a week so it's panic stations. The queues at each checkout are 20 deep and the trolleys are filled with eight litres of coke, a 48lb freak turkey, a 48 multibag of crisps, a sack of potatoes , 12 loaves of bread, a torch, some candles, maybe a flare and don't forget the Cadbury's Roses, Quality Streets , nuts and satsumas. Back to the lists, and without me saying anything I think the kids had picked up on the news story, well the girls had anyway. The boy was cracking on, his pencil was on fire. It was refreshing asking Harriet what she wanted, her list was as follows:

Some Babybels (cheese)
Some hammy (ham)
A 'warmy top'
A lollo (lolly)
A fi-fi
Some milky

Hatty would be delighted if we just wrapped up a pack of ham and a six-pinter of milk. It just comes down to food when you're a baby. I'm no humbug - I love giving out pressies but I definitely think we could survive without sets of bubble baths shaped as fruit or a Santa in a desert in a glass ball being fanned by a monkey. When everyone had finished we put Santa's address on the envelope and prepared to post them. It was a great sight, seeing them all beaming away, posting their lists in their pyjamas. Let's just hope the credit crunch hasn't reached Lapland. I may read this blog in the morning and think 'wow - delete, delete' as the old mind races a bit after games. I am now going to attempt to reduce the sweet mountain we still have after Halloween whilst watching late-night TV.

Danger

Day off today so a few of us players visited South Devon College for a bit of rehab/massage. Pete Morgan and his team battered and pummelled us, in a good way. I was fortunate enough to have a massage with Mel, who is incredible - real tears to the eyes stuff but very, very good. We are treated really well at the club and between Damien and Pete and the rest of the sports therapists, the care is excellent. Thanks also to Gareth, Jen, Tammy,

Amanda, Jodie and Charlotte who all pop into the club from time to time to give their help. I met my wife and The Beast (she is a very pretty beast!) afterwards and while my wife bought a few things, I took Hatty to a play centre to eat and dominate the place. It's always the same in these places and today was no exception. Hatty was playing and laughing as normal then while she was resting, a fellow player moved in for the kill. He thought no one was looking so he started launching plastic balls into Harriet's face from around one foot away. At first Hatty smiled. She was either thinking it was a game, or was thinking 'is that all you've got pal? It's gonna take more than that to defeat me'. On about the 15th strike to the face I had to step in and give the young lad the death stare, which had immediate effect. I looked round to see where his mum or dad might be. I found them when the boy in question had run back to base, crying 'she hurt me mummy'. His mum, who was elbow-deep in Now magazine, shot up to 'protect' the 'poor baby' and came over and spoke loudly: 'Try to play nicely everybody otherwise someone will get hurt'. The only chance of her boy getting hurt was if one the many missiles thrown were to ricochet of Hatty's face and roll onto him, rendering him poleaxed. It wasn't long before the mum was again eating the pages of Now magazine while the boy was ramming kids at top speed with a baby walker. We are all blinded by the love of our own kids though, and I'm no different. On one family holiday, my boy had managed to tame a real 'beach bully' after days of being battered. Cam had him floored. He looked up at me for instructions and the words that came out of my mouth were truly shocking. 'Finish him'. True to form the sand was displaced into the lads face and we walked back to our sun loungers victorious. That really was a massive one-off though, honestly. It's knowledge not power, that's the way forward.

I'm not feeling great at the moment. I would never admit to man flu but something has got me, and my body is rebelling today as I also got another big bang in the ribs last night. Whenever you don't feel great or have a 'knock' as a player your mood changes a bit. It really is 'bear with a thorn in his paw' stuff so do not approach or try to feed as it will pass. Really bad night's sleep as well. I finally nodded off at about 3am and the kids started getting up from about 6.30am. I don't know what's going on with my pillows at the moment but I'm having a real crisis. I must have lost my normal combination of two identical soft pillows during a house move but at the moment one pillow seems like a leaflet and two pillows seems like I'm resting my head on a cow. Fireworks tonight, come on!

THURSDAY, 6 NOVEMBER 2008

Awards

I have just been watching Sky Sports News and the managers of the month were being announced. League One's award went to Paul Trollope at Bristol Rovers. I was at Northampton Town with Troll and he is a great fella. At first the fans at the Cobblers were hard on Troll but true to character he carried on doing his job and deservedly won them over. When Colin Calderwood took over the club it suddenly became ultra-professional and myself and Troll thoroughly enjoyed playing there in our last season, and but for the most bizarre decision by a referee that I have ever seen in football we would have been rewarded with a play-off final, and the way we were playing probably promotion. I was surprised how soon Troll committed to management because he was very fit as a player, but the opportunity arose and he took it. With the help of Lennie Lawrence he has done extremely well with a tight budget. In fact when we played Rovers in pre-season, Troll was saying he had no assistant, no youth team and no physio and with 30 players looking at you for guidance it's a big ask. But he has a good manner about him and I think he will do very well. I have certainly had a broad spectrum of management styles over the years, having worked with 18 or so managers. All managers have to be motivators, it just depends on your style. At Brentford, Martin Allen had a fearsome reputation but he was actually just very committed and he certainly got the best out of his players, whether it be John Salako or a 17-year-old trialist. We had a great season the year I was there, finishing third at a club that had been tipped for relegation. Martin always looked after the players, we had a great trip to Dubai that Christmas, but what goes on tour stays on tour! Had the commute of five hours a day not have been killing me I would have stayed. Colin Calderwood was milder but no less committed. Then you have the old school-style, such as Alan Buckley and Jim Smith. I was with Alan at Grimsby and West Brom and if I had a spare week there would be many stories told. Maybe another time. I had plenty of run-ins with Jim, we certainly had our differences but it did make me smile seeing the old cigar smoke wafting down the team coach after games win, lose or draw. Here at Torquay, Paul Buckle is also a real motivator. He has created a great work ethic, he is approachable as a person but also has the respect of the lads as a manager. Training is very good, everything is done very professionally and we are all striving for the same thing.

FRIDAY, 7 NOVEMBER 2008

FA Cup

Time for the FA cup again and we are all looking forward to tomorrow's game against Evesham. They will be coming down to Devon full of confidence meaning we must be on our toes to avoid any problems. It is important to the club financially, and to the players it's always a great way of appearing on Match of The Day! I took the family to the fireworks at Plainmoor on Wednesday, great spectacle and a big turnout, but please no shouts of 'best display of the season'. The Hargreaves clan are going to another display with friends tonight so the kids can have their fix of sparklers, toffee apples and toys which break as soon as they get them home. Unfortunately I have been banned from having fireworks at the house. The last two years have been close shaves for different reasons. I admit there may have been a few slight safety breaches. One year when I had lit the new 'turbo rocket' it dislodged and flew past the kids about a foot away. The children loved it but my wife didn't as it found its way into the house through the patio door. The second incident was just bad luck, a combination of high winds and three of our guests finding a bottle of

Absinthe. Consequently I am banned from lighting anything this year. My wife even raises an eyebrow when I light candles at home but she can rest easy as our next-door-neighbour Dan is a fireman. Winner!

Happy birthday to Raiff Gwinnett, 18 this weekend. He brought a great selection of cakes in this morning, it put Toddy's 2-for-1 Mr Kipling's effort to shame. Raiff is a top lad, he takes a bit of a battering but it's all in good faith. A few square meals and he will be fine.

SATURDAY, 8 NOVEMBER 2008

Shocks

Torquay...2 Evesham...0. That's what the papers will say tomorrow morning, although credit to Evesham who really gave it a good go. We certainly were not at our best today but the FA Cup throws up shocks, so the important thing was that our result wasn't one. I am watching today's FA Cup highlights while typing away and as usual there were teams that came unstuck. Let's hope the second round draw is a good one. The players need to test themselves against teams in higher divisions, after all that's where we as a club want to be. Financially it goes without saying that a home and away tie against a big club and big crowd would be great. All that said, promotion is the main aim as far as I am concerned. Short blog today as I'm in a bad mood, a combination of tiredness and frustration about today's game. A big thanks today to all our supporters, much-needed support on a difficult day.

SUNDAY, 9 NOVEMBER 2008

Cheap as chips

So it's Oxford or Dorchester in round two of the FA Cup. Could be better, could be worse but it's at home, meaning we have a great chance of making it to round three and a potential money-spinning tie. Yesterday started early as normal, but for different reasons. My wife wanted to do a car boot sale with a friend so it was up with the lark and off for her. As soon as the door closed, Harriet arose shouting 'where's my mummy?' It was 6am. I actually attended the one other car boot sale my wife did but I was that traumatised I had to leave early. Queuing to get in, a ridiculous start time, crazy people attacking the car as you park up, and that's before you get to the selling. While I was there a woman approached us and picked up a pair of jeans. She haggled my wife down from around £10 to probably us paying her. That same pair of jeans that I was forced by my wife to drive all round London to find. It was for a club function at Brentford. That same pair of jeans cost more than a flight to Spain, by a long way. It's mayhem at car boots. You end up taking £1 for everything. 'How much for your car? I tell you what, I'll give you a quid pal!' Saying that, my wife made a small fortune yesterday. In the first 10 minutes she was offered £30 for a bag of jewellery by a man but a woman next to him said 'I was here first, will you take £80?' The man didn't get it. The rest of the stuff in the garage can go but there's that much in there it would take months of car boots. So bigger garage it is then. Yesterday I joined thousands of people all over Britain. Yes, tidying the garage has replaced going out with the lads to watch the footy or taking the motocross bike out. It involves shuffling around the garage in a bad mood and coming out two hours later having achieved nothing!

Last night I went to see the new Bond film. I was literally man-marked at the cinema for the whole night, firstly in the queue to get in. A couple were that desperate to get to their seat that I may as well have given piggy backs to both of them. Calm down, the trailers will last half an hour anyway! Then in my seat the bloke next to me was leaning that far across his seat into mine I thought about offering him my jacket to rest on. That one didn't last long though. The film was good. Bond escaped from the baddies, fell from a plane 10,000 feet into a crevasse and fought like a trooper but his collar was still always immaculate. He could fall into a rubbish tip and come out with a dinner jacket on, that's why he's James Bond. I was a bit disappointed with the villains in the film though, no dodgy teeth, bowler hats, piranha fish or spikes in boots anywhere to be seen. I also know that you were in there last night, you know who you are! I'll give you a clue. The heating was a joke, I lost around a stone in weight watching the film, people were dropping like flies in there. Even the chair tapper behind us stopped tapping to take his shirt off. Yes Dave (our driver) it was you, somehow you got into the building and turned the heating up to volcanic. Nice one!

Remembrance Day

Today being Remembrance Sunday we honour the millions who lost their lives in World War I and World War II. This morning I was reading an article about Clara Woodroffe, the mother who lost three of her sons on the battlefields of World War I. Only one of Clara's four sons survived because he was too old to fight. Her youngest son Sidney sent this letter to his mother from the trenches.

'Dearest Mother,

Here we are in the jolly old trenches! Thank goodness we are getting out of them tomorrow night. That will make nine jolly days of it, thanks very much. For one thing I shan't mind getting my boots off and changing my socks! Hooray too for a wash all over in (possibly!) warm water. I should like to go to a nice farm well away from the sound of guns and racket and miles away from this ghastly gas'.

Sidney never made it home. He was 19. Clara's second youngest, Kenneth, 22, sent this letter dated Boxing Day 1914.

'I am in a billet which is the only room left in a completely shattered village about 900 yards behind the trenches. Really mother, you people in England should just see what all this means. The church is in ruins, graves are blown up, the school is blown down and you can see the desks and books standing all ready for lessons. I had my first wash this morning since last Sunday. Everything is plastered in mud, I wonder if you would recognise me if I came home now, I doubt it'.

Kenneth was killed during the Battle of Aubers Ridge. Poignant letters which must have been extremely hard and upsetting for their mum to read. Conditions in the trenches were said to be so bad that during floods the soldiers were shoulder-deep in water. These two boys' graves were never found, along with 359,150 others whose battlefield graves were lost in further fighting. A total of 658,700 British servicemen lost their lives in World War I alone. Clara's other son, Leslie, lies in a grave in France. All the boys received honours - Sidney the Victoria Cross, Leslie the Military Cross and Kenneth was Mentioned in Dispatches. Clara lived until she was 89, a tough lady who suffered terrible grief but who it was said took some comfort from the medals of her boys. On Tuesday we have Remembrance Day again for those who fought and died in the 'Great War' and the 'Total War'.

OK, I know life has to go and until Tuesday I will stop talking about war. In tomorrow's blog I may talk about the 'standard' Sunday and car boot madness but for now it's roast beef, Yorkshire puds, roasties, mash, a few veggies and lots of gravy. Followed by sticky toffee pudding. Then it's Bond, James Bond, about £15 worth of plastic pick & mix, and a few litres of flat coke. If anyone throws popcorn I am liable to snap!

TUESDAY, 11 NOVEMBER 2008

Fight night

I drove in to training yesterday with Chris Todd. We got talking about Joe Calzaghe's fight with Roy Jones Jnr in New York on Saturday night. A great victory for Joe, especially after he had been knocked to the canvas in the first round. Toddy's brother James has turned pro and is now boxing out of Enzo Calzaghe's gym, a massive step towards making a name for himself. James was actually there on Saturday to watch the fight - in fact it turned out he was sat in the second row at the biggest fight of the year, not bad eh? It gets better. James was reading some programme notes when he looked up and turned to the left... he was sitting next to Coleen Rooney. He then turned to the right and... hello Mr Ricky Gervais! He turned round and clocked Danny De Vito! You know what it's like, you've gotta be seen in the right places! James was telling his brother about all this and asked Toddy why he hadn't answered his phone on Sunday morning. Toddy explained that he had fallen asleep, a bit of a shame really especially as James said that Joe wanted to speak to him after the fight. Chin up! When I was played for Oxford, Jim Rosenthal kindly gave me and three of the lads tickets to watch Calzaghe in Manchester. He was fighting Mikkel Kessler in what turned out to be a very tough fight. It went the distance and involved a lot of blood. On arrival at that fight we were approached by one of Jim's PA's who walked us into the massive MEN arena. To our shock we just kept going until the lady stopped and said 'there you are lads' - we were front row! So here we all were, me and the lads, Phil Taylor, Lennox Lewis and Amir Khan all mucking in on the front row! Joe Calzaghe won, and deservedly so. It was crazy being that close to the action, you could literally see the fear in the fighters' eyes. I think it must have helped him no end me shouting 'stay on your feet Joe, jab, jab!' A great night though. It must have been brilliant for James in Madison Square Garden on Saturday night, then mixing it at the after party with the big boys. Back to business and James' first fight is at the O2 arena on Saturday, 6 December, one for the diary. All of the Todds are decent boxers, even Mr Todd is considering a kickboxing career. On a recent stag night out for Toddy's other bro Liam, a mad man pulled out a blade and threatened the whole group of lads. Up stepped Todd senior who in a flash had floored him with a Kung Fu kick, go on Toddy's dad!

It turns out the mad man in question did have a knife... a butter knife. He may have to serve a few years inside for trying to 'spread' the lads. Back in Swansea, where home is, the Todd clan have been in a few scrapes, the highlight for me being the Christmas fancy dress night out that ended in a brawl. Some of the local bouncers tried to exert some unneeded force on the Todds. It must have been a great sight seeing Mrs Claus, an elf and Rudolf the red-nosed reindeer all getting stuck in. Chris is a great lad, the sort you would always have in your team. Unless it was a quiz team. Sorry mate, but the Blueberry shout yesterday was special. I just don't think Blueberry phones are out yet! Anyone interested in sponsoring Chris Todd's brother James, please contact the Herald Express Sports Desk.

Remembrance Day (again)

The 11th hour of the 11th day of the 11th month of 1918. This marked Armistice, the end of the World War I. Today, to honour those who died in both world wars and those who have died in action for their country since, we hold a two-minute silence at 11 a.m. Both world wars cost the lives of more than 1,000,000 British men. The facts about these wars are unbelievable. During the infamous Battle of the Somme, British casualties totalled 420,000. On the first day alone, 1st July 1916, there were 60,000 injured and 20,000 dead. This was the worst single day in British army history. When the battle was finally won in mid-November, Britain had suffered nearly half a million casualties, all this to gain five miles of land. Germany had 650,000 casualties and France 195,000. World War II was far more devastating in terms of loss of life. I was looking at some information about this war yesterday and the figures are truly shocking. Lithuania, Latvia and Germany lost more than 10 per cent of their populations. The Soviet Union and China both lost more than 20 million lives and Poland lost almost six million, 16 per cent of their population. The Holocaust alone resulted in the deaths of six million Jews. World War II, the 'Total War', involved 55 countries and between 1939 and 1945 a total of 72 million people had lost their lives. It makes grim reading I know but the freedom we have today is down to these young men and women who suffered beyond belief.

Hatty has just jumped on me and given me a big smacker and hug, a nice way to end the blog I think.

First Instalment

Super-quick post for now as time is of the essence. My wife has gone out, as soon as I arrived home in fact, and the children have destroyed the house so it's mayhem in the Hargreaves household. Harriet has just thrown a milkshake all over and is throwing tennis balls at me. The tennis balls were a recent purchase for yesterday's game between me and Dan (next door) and the score was 6-0, 6-1. Sorry mate, I had to get it in. Isabella is at athletics at 6.30pm but is currently making 'potions' in the bathroom. Cameron is at football at 6pm but has currently got three TVs on the go and I am currently trying to make a snack for them all while trying to find a black sock, a pair of leggings and my phone, which Hatty has been using. Got to go, it's all kicked off upstairs. Excuse me while I go and batter the kids!

Second Instalment

OK. Home now at 9.15pm so a bit more time to blog. Had training today in what has to be said were torrid conditions. Any more rain and we are going to have to train in Tesco's car park. The mood in camp is good, in fact Scott Bevan and myself are considering an approach from WWE wrestling. Our 'pumping iron' obsession has finally been recognised so don't be surprised to see a new tag-team on the box. Tarzan and the Bevanator are coming soon! Obviously we are focused leading up to the York game, a game that brings back memories of last season's play-off semi-final. No doubt it will be a tough test but we will be looking to win and keep up the momentum. I actually made my FA Cup debut for Grimsby at York... 19 years ago! I was 17-years-old and full of it. I'll take the same scoreline, a 2-1 victory with both goals coming from a short(ish)-haired lad called Chris Hargreaves. To be honest, the time actually has flown by in my career, and would I change it? Absolutely!

I would have stayed in and watched Match of the Day on Saturday nights instead of partying like Liam Gallagher. I would have stayed at some clubs for longer instead of making rash decisions. I would have left some clubs earlier instead of delaying decisions. And I wish I knew then what I know now. I think that's all called experience though and for now I will settle for success on the B-roads! I am going to have to go now as Danger Men: Red Arrows is on Channel 5 and I need to take in some more facts.

FRIDAY, 14 NOVEMBER 2008

Children In Need

I am relaxing my hotel room in Leeds watching Children in Need and thinking ahead to tomorrow's game against York, an important game that we are of course looking to win. I now have a new roomy in tow. With Chris Todd still injured and Wayne Carlisle on the treatment table, I welcome the latest victim, Michael Brough, with open arms. Broughy is a top lad who is obviously disappointed that he is not in the team at the moment. That aside, he is still as committed as ever in training, and fully behind the lads who are in the team. Yep, tea would be lovely Broughy - thanks mate! The trip up was, as usual, very long and very hot. We came by stagecoach and by the end of the journey there were parrots flying down the aisles. Needless to say, Nico has now gone for a refreshing shower. Our onboard entertainment consisted of a legendary game of Family Fortunes and the very long discussion regarding Elliot Benyon's mental state (it's unstable). I will reveal more about Family Fortunes at a later date. This evening's meal at the hotel was pretty good, a roast dinner followed by a bowl of Rennies. Looking forward to breakfast!

P.S. Cam and Issy - put those sweets away and stop driving mum mad. Love you crazy lot, see you soon - and as Del Boy would say... Bonjour.

Family Fortunes

I mentioned in Friday's blog that during the long journey to York we played a legendary game of Family Fortunes. Tim Sills, the games master, brought along the FF board game, the two 'families' were picked and soon it was hands behind backs, fingers on buzzers and those famous words 'We surveyed 100 people' kicked off the game. Family One consisted of Woods, Hargreaves, Benyon (someone had to have him), Mansell and Brough. Family Two consisted of Sills, Nicholson (those two were a banker to be on the same team), Hodges, Bevan and Adams. Nicky Wroe was the host - Bob Monkhouse, Les Dennis or Vernon Kay, whoever you prefer. And so we started: 'Steve meet Lee... Hi Steve... Hi Lee'. Name something you can read' etc etc. The early rounds were fiercely contested, then we came to 'Big Money' which we decided both teams would play in. Family One chose Hargreaves and Woods (we have experience and are sad enough to still be watching Family Fortunes on a Saturday night). Family Two chose Hodges and Adams (purely for banter). Woodsy went first while I put on the headphones and went into the booth (coach toilet). He did well, a few top answers and a good score. I followed and I've got to say was a bit nervous facing 'Bob', but it went well and a decent score had been set. Now up stepped Lee Hodges to face the questions. Here we go.

1. Name something you can play by yourself... you said 'cards'.
2. Name something you can polish... you said 'shoes'.
3. Name a pet that is easy to keep... you said 'dog'.
4. Name something that might follow the word 'don't'... you said 'do that'.
5. Name something a boss may give to an employee... you said 'a pay rise'.

The lads gave a small ripple of applause and the score wasn't bad. Up stepped Stevie 'Ghoul' Adams, an intelligent lad and a real gent.

'Steve, Lee did well - you need 97 to get the big money.
1. Name something you can play by yourself... 'football'
2. Name something you can polish... 'a bald head'.

47

3. Name a pet that is easy to keep... 'a biro'.
4. Name something that might follow the word 'don't'... 'cry'
5. Name something a boss may give to an employee... 'a bottle of wine'.

The buzzer we used nearly ran out of batteries it was pressed that much, and for only the second time in Family Fortunes history there was, surprisingly enough, no score. Stevie, let's break the answers down. Yes, if you like playing one-player football, shaking your own hand at the start and celebrating with your 'mates' when you have scored, then no problem. If you lose your hair in a few years and want to get the old Pledge out, then cool! If you are a little bit sensitive at the moment and think 'don't cry' is appropriate, that's fine. If you had your own business and wanted to give one of your staff a nice bottle of Claret, great. But if you think that an easy pet to look after would be a 'Biro' then I think we have got some serious issues. In your defence mate, you thought it was 'pen' not 'pet' and so I suppose 'Biro' would be a good pen to look after. It just shows you the pressure that these game shows can inflict on people. In fact, on a recent TV edition of Family Fortunes, when asked 'name a part of the body you can open, the panicked celebrity contestant answered 'a**e'. Say no more! Stevie, be prepared - next week Tim is bringing Mastermind.

Night shift – again...

Just returned home after a long trek back from York. It is 1.05am, all is quiet, I cannot sleep so it's time for late night TV and a few words on the blog. A great result *(won 2-1)* first and foremost. York hadn't lost at home this season. The team played very well and were rewarded with a big victory. Although the journey back was long, the banter was high quality, helped by a refreshment break mid-way. To have as many fans at the game as we did was a real boost, winning was the least we could do. The fact that it didn't rain must have been a bonus as well, uncovered away stands are not great. We looked a little bit different today due to our enforced shorts change. The ref seemed to think our light blue shorts clashed with York's dark blue shorts so something had to give. Instead of the home side changing to their away shorts as we had no spare set, they 'kindly' lent us their youth team's away shorts. Great effort with the old psychological games but it turned out that York beat York today. It didn't bother us at all, in fact we had a good laugh in the changing room watching some of our lads squeeze into those claret bad boys. No names mentioned but there were a few toffees being eaten in those shorts. My mum and dad were at the game, which was great, as was my old mate Michael Chapman. Sorry I couldn't stay over you guys but you know what it's like, a wrong move at this point could result in warfare at home. Couple that with the fact that the cost of a flight back had doubled, it was always going to be 90/10 against. I knew I should have booked that flight on Wednesday instead of trying to be clever and chancing it. I'm suddenly extremely tired, my body is rejecting all form of movement and I can hear someone stirring upstairs. I have to blog off. Please tell me Hatty hasn't sensed I'm home because if she has I am facing a night of torture. 1.45am and out.

MONDAY, 17 NOVEMBER 2008

Top to bottom

Top plays bottom tomorrow night as we host Lewes. On paper these games look easy but I can tell you they're not. Lewes will be scrapping for their lives. A victory for us would be just as important as it would against a team at the top. We will need to be on our toes big time when that whistle goes tomorrow. It always feels like a really long day when you play an evening game, it's a relief when finally the kit goes on and the warm-up starts. The day of a game, and the day before a game, feels much different to a normal day in that your mood changes and things become a bit more serious. The other difference is that when my mates are preparing to relax for the weekend or chill out at night, I am going to work - work that is stressful and emotional, and tough at times, but work that I know I am very privileged to be doing.

Bad times

I almost can't find the right words tonight. This isn't because there are no anecdotes or stories to tell, or that I'm tired or fed up. The reason is that I was told something tonight that shocked me in a big way. Early this evening I travelled to Plymouth to listen to a speech by Rob Walker, a freelance sports commentator. He has reported for the BBC1, BBC2, Channel 4 and Setanta. Most recently he was the sailing reporter at the Olympics and last Saturday you may have seen him commentate on the David Haye fight. I could talk about Rob all night – he's a real character. In tonight's speech his passion and enthusiasm about his media career and life shone through. It was great to speak to him briefly beforehand about football and boxing and I look forward to meeting him again. After listening to his inspirational and motivating words I jumped in my car to drive home. I made a quick phone call before I set off and bang... the words I am now struggling to find are about that conversation with a friend. I can't talk about it but what I can say is that in my life and probably many others we worry about jobs, contracts and money, we get stressed out with the kids or argue about bills. The thing that we take for granted is our health and our families and getting home to hug mine and tell them that I love them couldn't come soon enough.

TUESDAY, 18 NOVEMBER 2008

'Roomy'

Today, as you may have heard, the football club called a press conference. Present were Chris Todd, his mum and dad, partner Gemma and daughter Amylia. Also there were the chairman, manager, chief executive and myself. Chris Todd announced that he has leukaemia. This, he explained, had only been discovered on Monday when the news was broken to him. Toddy went on to explain a bit about the illness and his plan of attack. Further tests are to be done on Monday to find out more and to decide what form of treatment he will need. Together with his dad, Steve, he broke the news to his team-mates before last night's game which was obviously distressing and a real shock for the boys. It was surreal walking into a silent dressing room. Usually the stereo is blasting and the mood is high, but for a while it was very quiet. Through Toddy's bravery in talking to the lads and Paul Buckle's words afterwards, we all knew the job in hand had to be done - and it was. Tim Sills asked me in the warm-up if I thought lifting Toddy's shirt up would be appropriate, and it was - totally. It was fitting that Tim scored and raised it aloft. Today, as with last night, Chris Todd showed he is a true man, facing up to it, joking about it, and wishing the best for the lads. I have always had so much time for Toddy. He is a good laugh, as brave as a lion and a proper mate. The only thing that lets him down are his crazy tattoos, highlights and dress sense (only joking mate, can't wait to see Saturday's outfit). As he said today, and last night, he will deal with this illness like he has everything in his life - fighting all the way. I've no doubt Toddy will beat it and soon be destroying people on the pitch again like he has in the past. I actually phoned Chris on Monday night only 20 minutes after he had been told. My timing has always been shocking - he was very quiet and I'm not surprised. To be sat there watching TV one minute and then to hear you have leukaemia the next is not a normal experience but I couldn't think of anyone stronger to deal with it than Chris Todd.

To Chris, Gemma and Amylia, Steve, Julie and the rest of the Todd clan - we love you to bits mate and you know our thoughts are with you and your lovely family.

See you soon,
Greavsie and the lads.

THURSDAY, 20 NOVEMBER 2008

What a week...

What a week it has been. Toddy's news was a real blow and obviously nothing is more important than his recovery. He was cheering us on to victory on Tuesday evening, a victory *(4-1 away at Lewes)* that has broken records and put us to the top of the league. Although by recent standards we didn't play that well, the result was never in doubt. The only thing in the minds of the players and the management is trying to win games. After my last two seasons in football I won't be making any predictions. All I will be doing along with the rest of the lads is aiming to give the club and its supporters what they both deserve, which is league status. OK for now, I will sign off as I am taking my eldest daughter Issy to athletics. Cam, my son, is sat next to me shattered after covering some serious ground in a school match, as well as throwing a few 'Cruyffs', stepovers and chops into the bargain (yes, I know he is my son!). Harriet is 'helping' with the tea and my wife is giving me the glare because I'm sitting down, so as the Governor of California would say: 'I'll be back' .

Next Sitting

Just a few short words on this evening's activities. I played tennis with Dan (next door) again tonight. Come on, you know I'm going to mention it. It was tough, I was feeling tired and stiff. Dan had just been fighting fires for a few days. The score is not important Dan, it's the taking part. It's the banter, the fun. For the record, sorry again mate, I managed to scrape through in a close 6-2, 6-2 victory. I had one code violation for volleying (with my foot) a ball over the fence and onto a roof after a bad shot. I also had four code violations for offensive language, as did Dan! On the whole, it was a good game and as I said earlier (as long as you win) it's all about the taking part, the banter and the fun. See you on court next week mate. If you're still talking to me.

By the way, is that Timmy Mallet I see in the jungle? I met him after a game at Oxford, who he supports. As I'm sure you will see, Timmy is as mad as a box of frogs, but can he win it? If old Biggins can, anyone can (it's very doubtful though).

Maps and Legends

Here we are again. Another hotel, another away game (Woking), and hopefully another victory. The journey was, as per usual, horrific. Dave, our lovable driver, took us to London via Bristol, Northampton, Cambridge, and a small 'B' road that he discovered, which is not yet even on the Ordnance Survey map. Suffice to say the lads entered the hotel still in their sitting position having consumed 15 tins of travel sweets each. Normal service is resumed though – yes, my roomy is on the trip, and his card skills haven't improved. We are thinking of having an 'eat off' next week. The three main contenders are Michael Brough, Scott Bevan and Steve Adams. They have all shown, in the last 24 hours, extraordinary appetites, Stevie Adams in particular. His 'Sport Billy' bag contains a surprising quantity of snacks. Three hours into today's journey he produced a whole cooked chicken! Got to get some sleep now, so speak soon.

SUNDAY, 23 NOVEMBER 2008

London Town

At the final whistle in yesterday's match against Woking, the general feeling in the changing room was one of frustration with a 2-2 draw. Before the game we were confident we could win and at the end of the game we thought we should have won. Obviously at half-time and at 2-0 down, a draw would seem like a good result, but we were that dominant in the second half that it felt a bit disappointing that we hadn't taken all three points. I spoke to Phil Gilchrist, their manager, after the game and he was more than happy with a point. The ground pretty much felt like it had been taken over by Torquay fans, which again was a massive bonus. So with the game over, the squad travelled into London for the annual (if early) Christmas do. It was back to the hotel first though to change into the old dancing gear. Once the boys had showered and shaved it was straight to the tube station and into Covent Garden. We spent a few hours there before heading to clubland. First it involved a quick taxi ride to the Met Bar on Park Lane (I'll come back to that), then on to another club back in the West End. Most of the lads were already queueing when our taxi arrived. The queue was big, it was cold... so why not! Yep, I nipped to the front of the queue and began the blag. Our names had been put on the guest list but when I asked the guys at the door it was a negative. It may have been the sight of 10 or so of the lads at the back of the queue livening proceedings up that suddenly erased the names from the list. Time for Plan B. 'Come on, the lads have travelled up a long way, don't let them down – we'll be little angels in there', Smile and wait... the rope was lifted and to the annoyance of the freezing hopefuls in the queue, the boys marched past and into safety. As usual, the clubs were a frenzy of celebs, wannabes and footballers. Understandably there weren't many takers for the first round. The remaining kitty was swallowed up in minutes rather than hours due to the price list at the bar. It was that bad that the bar staff gave you a tissue and a 'get well soon' card after each order. It could have been much worse though. As I said earlier, we had already been to the Met Bar, kindly sorted by 'Hells Bells' (Helen Chamberlain) but it was early and a bit quiet in there so we moved on. But I had told Damo, Kenny, Bri and Shaun we would meet them in there, only remembering when I received a text from Damo saying he had just come round after paying £50 for four drinks. Smelling salts, anyone? Back to our watering hole and one of the lads was having a bit of banter with a couple when the guy said 'tell you what, I'll get a bottle eh, then you get one. OK?' The waitress came over and beamed. 'That's £400, thanks.' Shoulder officially dropped at that point. Don't mess with bottles of Crystal is the lesson there. It didn't stop plenty in there though, there were that many ice buckets with sparklers it was like fireworks night. What with the ice sculpture and the chocolate fountain, the credit crunch was nowhere to be seen. I have to say though, I love London - the sights, the restaurants, the buses and black cabs and the town houses in squares overlooking little parks. I know for a day trip or a weekend it's a novelty but I think I could live in London quite happily, as long as I had a few million in the bank. The ideal scenario is a home in Devon and a pad to crash in London for the odd blast. But for now it's the odd day or evening like last night. A great laugh, a little cameo role by Phil Mitchell off Eastenders, a 10-man race on rickshaws and a faultless man-marking display by one of the lads and the night was over. Is that the alarm clock? We've only just got in!

Shop 'til you drop

Today I tried to go shopping with the girls - my wife and daughter - but again I failed. Fiona wanted to buy a few things so I entertained Hatty, but I was beaten both mentally and physically. Physically, 10 yards of being in her buggy and it's 'shoulders daddy'. The old body starts to creak after carrying 'H' for 30 minutes. Mentally there are only so many shops you can be led into and asked 'what do you think about this one? Is it really me?' Harriet tried her best as well. She entertained the Xmas shoppers by waving and dancing from inside the window displays, but after an hour (and that included coffee) we were both broken so we abandoned ship and returned home, leaving Fiona to shop and relax for a few hours.

I was asked recently by a friend if I wanted to try the Paris-Dakar rally. As much as I want to, it's difficult while I'm playing football and judging by Charley Boorman's (of Long Way Round) retirement in a recent rally due to a broken hand (he fell off his bike) it's pretty dangerous too. The journey is mammoth, around 5,000 miles, and dangerous. This year's rally was cancelled because of the danger in Africa, and will now take place in South America in January 2009. As with all the adventures that I fancy doing, they are firmly on the back burner for a few years yet (hopefully). It doesn't stop me plotting and planning though. Everest, the London Marathon, the Amazon, even surviving an afternoon's shopping with the girls are all challenges ahead. One adventure that may not take place is a one that another friend of mine recently completed. The annual Mont Blanc 100-mile run is not one for the faint-hearted. It basically is a non-stop, yes non-stop, run over ridiculous mountainous terrain in as quick a time as possible. Rob completed the run in around 40 hours. He said he was hallucinating towards the end and that stopping for a drink six or so miles before the end was a big mistake. The last few miles, uphill, took about seven hours. A great achievement and a very emotional finish, I'm sure, for him and his waiting family.

TUESDAY, 25 NOVEMBER 2008

Another day at the office

Super-quick blog as I'm very busy today. Training this morning was excellent. The lads came in after a few days off and really put it in. We had a keep-ball session that was fiercely contested, then we went into a game. It was played at full tempo with tackles, shots and headers flying in. The morning session was rounded off with a few sprints, all the boys being flat out at the end. Then it was into the gym for a blast on the weights (all the best with the golf tomorrow, Kev). I have to say the attitude of the whole squad was spot on, that's the way we all want it to be for the rest of the season - a togetherness and team spirit that will hopefully carry us through.

I'm thinking about having guest bloggers on and it may start tonight. As well as this, throughout the course of the next few weeks I will be giving you a little bit of info on each player - loves, hates etc. so watch this space. Speak soon.

Court out...

No guest blog tonight as kids have gone to bed and my wife is online job hunting (again!!).

Newsflash: On to tonight's tennis now - game, set and match Chris Hargreaves, 6-2, 6-2, 18 code violations shared between two players including 12 uses of bad language, four volleying of tennis balls with feet and two cases of clothing abuse (Dan). See you next week mate, with a new racket.

Toddy's Blog

When Greavsie asked me to do this I was so happy to say yes... So where do I start? What a crazy and life-changing week. I would first like to thank everyone from the bottom of my heart for the support I have received. It has touched me in so many ways. I don't think I have ever had so many frogs in my throat and I don't mean the ones out of water. I will say this - I have grown up so much in the last few days, it has made me realise so many things about life that normally I would take for granted. Believe me, if everyone realised that one phone call could do this they would most probably look at life with a whole different outlook. The club have been amazing and have helped me in so many ways already. I have the best manager a player could wish for and his class backroom staff with him. A physio who has not left my side, and who will be a big part in getting me healthy. A keeper coach who does just about everything at the training ground. And Northy for winding me up all the time about the Welsh. The lads have been a great help in keeping me smiling, not with their banter as it needs some work, especially Greavsie ha ha. On a serious note they keep me going and are true friends. With the support I am getting from everyone around the world I hope and believe I will be back on the pitch in a yellow shirt very soon!

Chris Todd

Big Money Round?

It's the evening before the match against Oxford, the second round of the
FA Cup. We need to progress to the third round where hopefully a big club
awaits, and some much needed £££££. I have played in lots of FA Cup
ties over the years, lots of highs and some lows. Highs include goals for
Grimsby, Northampton, Hull, Plymouth and Brentford and others, and
lows include a goal for Man Utd. Yes, I did say a goal for Man Utd. It was
during a great cup run with Northampton. We had beaten Rotherham away
in the fourth round and were drawn against Man Utd at home. The club
actually made over £1million from that cup run. Unfortunately I scored an
own goal, just after half time and at 1-0 down, against the current
champions. In over 600 games it was, and still is, the only own goal I've
scored. A viewing audience of 60million worldwide, about 30 family and
friends at the game and a party arranged for the night... brilliant! I couldn't
wait to do the press after that game. The only good thing that came out of it
was that I gave Nicky Butt a bit of a slap for a late challenge. Another
moment in the FA Cup, this time enjoyable, was a goal I scored for
Plymouth (in the right end this time) at Reading in the third round. We
were losing 1-0 when in the last few minutes I managed to smash one in the
top corner. Off came the shirt, I ran around the goal and celebrated in front
of about 4,000 travelling fans. My brother was in the crowd that day and he
said it was a great buzz when the goal went in as a bloke who jumped on
him to celebrate had a Hargreaves shirt on. They did sell one that year then!
As I have said before, it is a great chance for players to appear on Match of
the Day. I will have to try and locate those old videos some day.

Home Time

Shattered! A great victory today, beating my old team Oxford 2-0 and with 10 men. We were a bit tentative in the first half but scored a good goal before the break. Unfortunately we also lost Roscoe D'Sane to a harsh sending off. But with 10 men we rolled the old sleeves up and actually looked the more dangerous team in the second half, topping off a great display with a second goal to win the game. Well done to all the boys, they gave it everything, and along with some good tactical decisions it was a well-deserved result. We certainly needed our fans today and they didn't let us down, great support in freezing conditions. I think I tempted fate in last night's blog, talking about scoring an own goal in an FA Cup tie. It nearly happened again today. I was trying to defend a cross and headed the ball towards goal, but Scotty Bevan made a good save and it was panic over (that's what keepers are paid for anyway). What with the own goal scare, and nearly walking out with Matt Green's shirt on before the game, it was a relief to be sat in the changing room after the game, victorious and with the right shirt on. I am now sat watching X-Factor with an ice pack on, the kids are playing Junior Monopoly with their grandparents and we have all just destroyed an Indian takeaway and a few bottles of red. Bliss!

Draw

Double shattered! No sleep at all last night, a combination of too much caffeine in the system and a new duvet that pushed the room temperature up to around melting point. This morning I dropped my son off at football with his grandad, the girls stayed at home with grandma and my wife and I drove to the club for a bit of lunch and to listen to the FA Cup third round draw. Along with a few of the lads and their partners we all waited in anticipation.

'*Number 56… Torquay United*' Come on Ray Clemence, say Man Utd; come on Ray, say Arsenal '*…will play Blackpool*'.

I never really took to Ray Clemence and I can see why now. It could be worse though, it could be away to Blackpool. Joking aside, it's not a Premiership club which everybody had hoped for but it is a game that we can win, for now though it goes well and truly on the back burner. On returning home it was time to get serious. Out came the Christmas decorations and for the next three hours we set about the house in true Christmas spirit. The Christmas CD went on, the baubles were thrown all over, each room had the 'full works', and that many lights have been rigged up that Dan (next door) will have to do a full safety check (he's a fireman) before they are turned on. Time to chill out in front of the TV now, and it's a BBC2 fest. I'll be watching The Long Way Down, Top Gear, Louis Theroux and then Match of the Day… if my wife lets me. Very doubtful.

MONDAY, 1 DECEMBER 2008

Issy and Cam (guest blog)

Issy: On Sunday we got the decorations out, and without dad getting frustrated we made the house look great. Hatty was wrecking the Christmas tree and standing on the baubles. I went upstairs with tinsel and lights and decorated my bedroom as well. I am looking forward to Christmas so much. I want it to be every day. Can't wait to break up from school and have peace and quiet. For Christmas I would like a big dressing table to put all my bits and bobs on.
Cam: Hi there! Dad has just broken the garage door. I can't get my bike out, my footballs out or anything else that I want. Grandad came to see me play football on Sunday, luckily we won 2-1. Issy has been yapping away telling me what to write and it is getting quite annoying. I went to watch dad on Saturday, it was a bit rough. Soon we are going to be doing the Christmas play, I am taking on the part of Joseph so I need to learn my

lines soon. My birthday is on Thursday, it's been a nightmare waiting. I have just started my advent calendar, today I woke up to a big piece of chocolate behind the door of number one!

Testing Times

I can't believe I managed to watch a whole episode of 'I'm a Celebrity, Get Me Out Of Here' without throwing the control through the TV screen. My anger levels watching the box these days are really worrying me. My wife already thinks I'm a cross between Jim Royle, Victor Meldrew and Jack Nicholson in 'As Good As It Gets', who basically is wound up by everything and only likes a few things. I know watching the jungle antics can be addictive, but watching last night I was cringing at the pleas for votes by the celebs and the total 'wetness' of Brian Paddick, who reached the top in a hard profession but who on the show came across like a proper wet blanket. He stood there hanging on every word from a singer from Blue and an Eastender. Get a grip mate! As for the other inmates, purely on her huge achievements and also the fact that she is a lovely person I won't have Martina Navratilova criticized. Fair play to Simon Webbe, who tried to conquer his obvious fears in the water trial but who milks the old 'righteous' one. George Takei surely doesn't speak in Star Trek mode all the time, Nicola McLean's chest is going to blow up if she goes to close to the fire and Joe Swash is more Cockney than Chas and Dave. Finally we have David Van Day - love him or hate him, he is pure entertainment and is a dead cert for the baddie in panto as soon as he steps out of the jungle. Worst of all though are the adverts during the show. Someone needs shooting for hiring Kerry Katona for the Iceland ads. I don't mind old Biggins, but no I don't want a box of 12 king prawns complete with plastic spoons and I'm not going to do the conga eating a frozen vol-au-vent.

I have been tested to the max this morning by my awesome little two-year-old daughter. I know what Fiona feels like now being home alone with Hatty. This morning started early and went something like this. 'Read daddy'. Ten books later it was 'den daddy'. A displaced disc later and 'I'm hungry daddy'. Her menu was scrambled egg followed by some cheese, then two yoghurts, a bottle of milk, a lolly (couldn't help it, she found it!) and three advent calendar chocolates (never going to get to Christmas). Along with the food she wanted to watch cars on TV and also came out with lots of mental phrases, including 'oh dod almighty', 'I go to work now', 'I won't blue jeans on', 'don't annoy me daddy', 'don't wind me up', 'I lub you daddy', 'here's your hair clip daddy', 'I need some sheese' and five cries of 'I need milk daddy, NOW'. She is now across my lap with the TV control down her top, wincing while eating some Kiwi fruit. Life is good but please Fiona, come home - all is forgiven.

Game tonight and the same as normal is required - a win.

WEDNESDAY, 3 DECEMBER 2008

Express Delivery

Late blog due to a non-stop day, this being the first time I have sat down - at 9.55 pm. Last night we lost 1-0 to Forest Green, and the reaction? No-one likes losing but hopefully the positives of being out of that competition will far outweigh the negatives - i.e. fixture pile-up. I had the pleasure of watching the lads last night and they put in a really professional performance, some after not playing much football at all this season, and although the result wasn't great the attitude was. Thanks to Mrs Mansell and clan who looked after us at the match, much-appreciated food, warmth and banter.

Today I have been given gifts by mates and this is unusual for me. I met a friend for lunch, who kindly gave me two things, firstly food, secondly - and more importantly - his advice, thanks mate. Then another friend of mine gave me a great early birthday present for my boy, Cam, and the beauty is we can both use it! Nice one. Got lots flying around in my mind tonight but if I start going off on a tangent and blogging it, two things will happen - I won't sleep and you will turn the computer off, so goodnight and God bless. Oh, just two facts then...

1. 80 billion text messages sent worldwide every day

2. Very cold tomorrow!

04/12/1998

Happy Birthday Cam Hargreaves, 10 years old today. Cam is my Mini-Me, a little best mate and I love him so much. His nicknames are Miggy, Nambins, T-bear and Manbear. A father-and-son relationship that is dominated by kick- ups together, winding each other up and lots of hugs. We got Cam a new bike for his birthday as he had worn his other one out. As well as that, he got some clothes, the obligatory computer game, footy boots (like the lads wear!) and an under-armour. Yes, even at 10, all the young football starlets have to have the designer thermals. Issy got him a chocolate football boot but Harriet got hold of his tube of smarties and started destroying them at 8am. Not a bad day for the boy all in all, especially with Christmas to come.
The kids also received their replies from Santa this morning (typed by the elves) so they are excited. Santa may well visit again this year but when he does I (I mean he) seems to take on a Welsh accent. Must work on that one. Not forgetting the year Santa, after visiting us, was locked out of the house for half an hour with only a pair of shorts on. Crossed wires and too much consumption of wine by my wife to blame for that one.

My Christmas memories as a boy are littered with bizarre events. Losing my brother's bike on Christmas Day was a bit worrying, but having the only customised chopper in the street (a glitter spray job) on Xmas day wasn't bad. Another time I was fooled into thinking my new remote control car had a lead on, so you had to walk it like a dog. It wasn't great (mum, I bet you're laughing now - I know it was payback for me being the devil's child). But when the joke was over, an hour later, on Xmas morning, and my real car was revealed - a Corvette Stingray - I blasted it round the neighbourhood for the rest of the day using about 20 batteries and traumatising my brother, who had chosen a truck and trailer that crept along at about 0.5 mph. Your reversing was awesome though mate!
Great times, but I got up to so much mischief back then my mum and dad must have gone stir crazy. It was all worth it in the end though, especially now some of the restraining orders have been lifted.

FRIDAY, 5 DECEMBER 2008

Fun and Games

We have a great game to look forward to tomorrow. Cambridge at home is a going to be a stern test but one that we are ready for. A return to a league game and hopefully back to winning ways. Update on club gamesmaster Tim Sills' TV appearance. Forget 'Don't Forget The Lyrics', that dream is over, but say hello to 'Wogan's Perfect Recall'. Yes, the Quizmaster Funk is at it again but this time it's for real. The date? 17 December. The day? Wednesday. The contestant? T Sills. And the show? 'Wogan's Perfect Recall', a game show on Channel 4 that requires contestants to show off their memory and general knowledge with prize money of up to £250,000 on offer. One for the diary there.

Starter for 10 points - how much money will go into the players' fund if Tim hits the jackpot? Answer from Tim: 'You're breaking up mate, gotta go, I'm having Terry over for drinks'.

Second bombshell of the day, revealed in the weekly circle. Up steps a great lad, everyone's friend, a real gent - Kev Nicholson. And the revelation? He woke up this morning racked with guilt about a dream, a 'liaison' with one of the lad's wives. We're thinking 'come on Kev, it can't be that bad, it happens'. Then the revelation. 'It was Fiona Hargreaves'. Brilliant. Thanks for that mate. To be fair though, the lads' reaction was very funny. That reminds me, I really did enjoy those Exmouth days. Kev's fiancée Jenny, me and the strawberries... oh, and Kev walked in and ruined it!

Sunday

Yesterday's game *(0-0 at home to Cambridge)* could, and maybe should, have been won as we were the side who had the most chances. The reward of one point for all the effort the lads put into the game seems harsh but we know that in the last couple of months, performances and results have been excellent so, as I always say, we go again - starting on Tuesday at Eastbourne.

Very light blog tonight as the last 40 minutes writing a story about a family trip to Eastbourne have been in vain. The Beast has just ripped the phone plug out of the socket, I hadn't pressed save, the battery was dead and so as they say 'it's a goner'. That reminds me, is it bedtime for my little angels? I will double blog late on Tuesday night when me and the Red Bull get home.

Brighton Pier

Arrived at our hotel last night after a journey of ridiculous length and heat. To rub salt into the wounds, I was sandwiched in between Mark Ellis and Dave the driver for our evening meal. The banter was very poor. I asked Dave to pass the water and he looked over to the sea and said 'there's plenty out there'. And Mark just stared at us as if he wanted to eat us both. We are situated on Brighton seafront, so it's a banker for hitting Brighton Pier today.

WEDNESDAY, 10 DECEMBER 2008

Move on

It has been a long time - in fact I think it's the first time - I have posted on the blog after having played in a game in which we lost *(4-2 at Eastbourne)*. I haven't talked in great detail about the wins and so I won't about the losses. What I will say is that there are no excuses. We definitely didn't play well and we didn't deserve to win. First and foremost, as captain I look at my own performance and I am far from happy. I am certainly not going to criticise my team-mates, their efforts in the last few months have been massive. As a team we will look at what went wrong tomorrow morning in training. We have to make sure this is a one-off and go out to win the next two games, the first on Saturday against Bath and the second the following Saturday against Histon. Finally I have to say thanks to the supporters who travelled to Eastbourne to watch. I know it wasn't the display and result you were hoping for. Returning home at 4am this morning after losing has put me in the sort of bad mood that won't be lifted until we are sat in a winning changing room once again. This may all sound like boring old spiel but I am not in the mood for cartwheels. I know that you have to move on though, and quickly, starting with watching the kids' performance in the school play at 2pm this afternoon. No comments, please, on who will play the donkey.

Nativity

This evening we were treated to another performance of the Christmas play. It was very good, a classic nativity play. The children have been in some bizarre Christmas plays at different schools before. I remember one play in Northampton being set in space and lasting for over one and a half hours. Stick to the original format, we want to see Mary and Joseph, three kings, baby Jesus and the innkeeper and his wife, job done. And so it was. As well as being super-quick (it lasted 30 minutes), the play ticked all the boxes, and bonus points for Cam, our son, as he was Joseph. He remembered all his lines but he refused to hold hands with Mary and was a bit intimidated by her size (a foot difference). Isabella was spitting feathers in the back row, she was only an angel. To make matters worse, Cam was given a box of chocolates after the play. More bribes needed for next year's lead parts, I think. I managed to video the show, which was no mean feat considering the size of the camcorder I was holding. We bought it over 10 years ago and times have moved on. People watching the play thought the BBC were in filming a documentary, the camera was that big. I dread to think what the film looks like as I had the shakes for the final scene, my forearm was failing. Still I shouldn't worry, Cam's first birthday (he is 10 now) is still on a tape in the box with all the other plays, weddings, Christmases, birthdays, holidays, and bar mitzvahs that we have filmed over the years with that camcorder. It's a miracle I found the box with the camcorder in. The amount of house moves we have had recently have meant that some boxes have remained unopened for years on end, going from garage to garage. Which reminds me, I must remember to look for the box marked 'kids' pets'. Only joking - they are safe and sound at friends in Northampton. Hi to Flopsy the rabbit - if you have managed to unlock the gate, open the back door, turn the computer on... oh, and have learnt to read!

Wembley trail

Our journey, hopefully to Wembley, has started today after our 2-0 victory against Bath. It has certainly been a long week though, and sat here now looking back at the last few days all I can say is I think the lads will really benefit from some time off. Being away from football to recharge the batteries, to spend some time with family and friends, can be important. Then it's back in, ready to train well and ready to beat Histon. Personally I am a bit worn out at the moment. A combination of not feeling great and also having played 30 or so games already may have something to do with it. It is a long season and at the moment I am in pain, but a few good nights' sleep and some good food will sort it out. As well as feeling rough, I am not totally happy with my game. Like a lot of players, unless you are putting in man-of-the-match performances every game it's frustrating, but after all these years I know it can soon turn. I still have goals that I am aiming for, none more than promotion with Torquay, so it's a case of head down, dig in and most importantly win at all costs. Tonight, like millions of others, it's X-Factor for me, and tomorrow it's a Christmas party for the kids, then a trip to Bristol to watch Toddy's bro hopefully win his first pro fight.

MONDAY, 15 DECEMBER 2008

Fight Night

I travelled up to Bristol with Chris Todd last night to watch his brother, James, fight, and what a night it was. James is now fighting out of the Calzaghe gym and last night was his first professional fight. Along with Wayne Carlisle, his clan, and our mate Barry we eventually sat down for the pre-fight meal. Oh, I forgot to mention the 30 or so Todd family members and friends who descended on the Thistle hotel, a regular Bristol boxing venue, ready for action after their journey from Wales. The three tables filled were certainly going to create some noise. For a bit of extra muscle, throw in Enzo Maccarinelli as well who joined the group. We all had a good chat before the fight, even James popped in to say hello. The last time I had seen him was a few months ago at training and he looked a different person. He had dropped a few pounds to get in at the weight of 10st for a light-welterweight, but he looked fit and ready. Onto the fighting, and the first two bouts were decent but we were all keen to see James in action. It was a long wait for his family and friends though, when after these first two bouts the master of ceremonies announced that the auction would start. A few signed gloves, signed shirts and a couple of grand later it was time for the two fighters to enter the arena. James came in to a great reception. It was a great sight seeing him bowl in wearing the Todd number six Torquay shirt. He jumped into the ring looking strong and ready. Then his opponent came in - Adam Cunningham, a local lad, also to a great reception. A quick check and chat by the referee and the bell was sounded, four three-minute rounds. Here we go. It started ferociously and before you knew it, pretty much all the punters were standing up with the shouts of 'Toddy, Toddy' ringing around the place. It was a great fight, both of the lads were full-on. I can't remember a lull in any of the rounds. James moved round the ring brilliantly and rained in some great combos. He actually looked stronger as the fight went on, I reckon he could have done another four rounds. The bell sounded for the end of the fight and the two sets of supporters obviously thought their own fighter deserved the victory. We all obviously thought James took it because of his finish to the fight, the Bristol supporters thought it was their man, home advantage and all. And the result? A draw. It was a big decision, the first two rounds were given to Cunningham, the second two given to Todd. I can tell you that there would have been a near riot if victory had gone either way. Toddy was gutted, his family and friends were gutted, but were also really proud as their boy had gone in there and really fought well. Both the lads were given glowing reports by the ringmaster, who said he would be very surprised if neither of them went on to fight for a British Championship at some point. I went to see James after the fight to say well done. He was in the dressing room with another 'away' fighter, who to be fair had been battered in the last bout of the night. It reminded me a lot of football dressing rooms after defeats when you're shattered and annoyed and you just want to get out and go home to lick the old wounds. James was disappointed he hadn't won, he deserved to, but he must have been pleased with his first pro fight. His family and friends certainly were. James is 19, the lad he fought was 32 and had 60-odd amateur fights under his belt. It was a great performance from Toddy and I think the lad he fought will definitely be pleased with a draw today.

TUESDAY, 16 DECEMBER 2008

Old mates

In the 20 years that I have been playing football, I have come across some great characters and made lots of friends. Unfortunately the fact that I have had more clubs than Tiger Woods means that staying in regular touch can be hard. You know what it's like, up at 7am with the kids, school run, training, coaching, athletics, dinner, homework etc - its all go. I only just have time to argue with my wife before we sit down to relax about 9 pm. So the thought of then making/receiving a long phone call can be a bit of a killer, especially when you are allergic to phones calls like I am. My mates are used to my phone phobia excuses – 'it fell in the bath', 'my son keeps losing it' (that one lasted four years), 'the battery is dead', 'the signal is rubbish', 'I left it up north' (for two weeks). Imagine what I'm like with calls I don't recognise. In fact, I have seriously considered sending my phone to friends abroad in the summer when I'm off. Ringing with a foreign dialling tone would definitely put people off and may buy me a couple of weeks of peace. It's not that I'm anti-social, I just don't like people. Only joking, I love meeting people. Just not on the phone. I once struck up a great friendship with a stockbroker who was anti-phones while on hols in the Caribbean. Our respective girlfriends/wives were busy with the Hawaiian Tropic. You know the one, eight hours already in the baking heat and if you step near them 'you're blocking the sun, I'm in your shadow'. So being restless anyway, and having walked up the nearest mountain and having nearly drowned two miles out to sea, I crept away. Luckily for me, I met this great bloke at the bar who ignored his phone as if it was poisonous. He introduced me to Gin and Tonic (I've never looked back) so most afternoons for us two were then taken care of. We were also both safe in the knowledge that our partners were still welded to their towels, hooked up to a drip of factor 10 and committed as ever to their Sun God. Whenever I go away with my mate Daryl Burgess and his family, we have a great laugh when our wives rise up off the sun loungers to have a dip. In typical David Attenborough lingo '...and here we have the female of the species venturing down to the watering hole, it's best not to approach at this stage as they can be extremely dangerous...'. Anyway, there is a point to this story. Phones can be used for speaking and not texting. I actually phoned my mate Daryl back last night as he had left a message (no answer from me again) saying he needed my new address for Christmas cards etc. I was with Daryl at West Brom and Northampton, our families have been away lots of times together and have had some great laughs, although our last holiday was this summer just gone, two weeks in a haunted villa in the middle of nowhere in torrential rain... hilarious! We have been in caravans (no comments, please), had trips to St Tropez, Puerto Pollensa, and in fact most of Spain. It was great to catch up and talk about old times and stories, some of which I may talk about soon (yachts, David Dunn, bizarre circus acts, and fluorescent rain coats in Prague to name a few) but for now I am going to have to go as I think the girls have destroyed the top floor of the house. Oh, and while I have been writing this, the home phone has rung three times and my mobile has rung twice. Come on, I've been busy!

Jammin'

It has been a couple of days since I have written on the blog so apologies there. We had a nice little jamming session at the club this morning. Big performances were put in by Wayne Carlisle and, from nowhere, our part-time fitness coach, Fletch. Beforehand, as a bit of a warm-up, the trainees gave us a few renditions of well-known Christmas carols with Grant giving a nice solo and Steve throwing some hardcore shapes into the bargain. Onto the main event, and with Wayne having had his old guitar replaced with a spanking new one he was 'encouraged' by senior management to try it out. For a bit of guidance and encouragement, Fletch offered to sit in and he just happened to have his guitar and full list of songs in his car this morning... Lead vocals went to Damien Davey, with Tim Sills on backing vocals (surprisingly Tim was reluctant to join in at first, his best work is obviously done at night). What a gig it was. We were treated to cameos of Oasis, Paulo Nutini and the Stereophonics, to name but a few. Wayne's guitar playing was great (bearing in mind it was his first gig in front of anyone - he told me was more nervous than before any game). The singers were spot on as well, but it has to be said that Fletch came into his own with both guitar and voice. He actually made me jump when he joined in (took over) from the lads halfway through one of the songs and belted out the remainder of the track like an old pro (the fact he is in a local band may explain it). Top stuff though, a great start to the day. Training followed which involved final preparation for our game against Histon tomorrow, a big game, and a game that we are looking to win. Finally, the head tennis duo of Hargreaves/Woods has now become a trio. A third member has been recruited and welcomed with open arms. His ability to abuse match officials, dispute all line calls and generally win at all costs impressed the judges enough to claim his place. Yes - Lee Hodges, come on down! And the first game as a three (three games up to 21 points)? Results as follows:

*Hargreaves, Woods, Hodges...*3
*Mansell, Robertson, Nicholson...*0

I'm keeping it quiet, but Manse and Robbo want a new member. It's getting a bit much for Kev.

Next Please

Nearly forgot - in other news, the newly formed 'Book Club' (OK, it's only me and Broughy, we were very bored at a service stop the other week) has finished its first book. The book was called 'City Boy' and is basically the account of a (now ex-) City boy on the scandal, wrongdoing and massive misuse of money that has resulted in the mess we find ourselves in today, i.e. trillions of pounds of debt. Great book, great banter, worrying pension fund!

SATURDAY, 20 DECEMBER 2008

Winning Ways

Back to winning ways today in the league, and in style. A 4-1 victory against Histon feels and looks good. We can really kick on from here and assert ourselves on this league. With the support we get each week from our fans and the ability and desire we have in the squad, I know it can be a great season. That's it! No stories, no anecdotes. I hope everyone reading this has a top night and I will resume with my normal behaviour tomorrow.

SUNDAY, 21 DECEMBER 2008

Meldrew

The countdown to Christmas is here so it's lots of Celebrations (the sweets), tangerines and nuts to get through and plenty of old-school films on the TV. In fact, as I am typing away, ET is on in the background, as usual playing to no-one as the kids can't sit still long enough to watch anything. My wife is in bed ill (a smokescreen I think, so she didn't have to get up early with Harriet, take the children out or cook the dinner). I might actually go upstairs soon and quietly rush in, I'll probably find her relaxing eating

Belgian chocolates whilst reading Hello magazine. Anyway, me and the rest of the clan headed to the beach this morning to blow the cobwebs away. Twenty rolls down the sand dunes later we were ready for refreshments, especially as the 'Devon Dog Beach Meeting Society' was beginning to grow in number. I like dogs and eventually we will get one, but when there's an 8ft Great Dane bounding towards my little girl looking like it hasn't eaten in weeks, it's definitely time to go. To be fair, its owners were shouting the obligatory 'don't worry, he doesn't USUALLY bite, he's a big softy', but I couldn't take the risk. Harriet could have got away with riding it as a back marker at the Grand National, it was that big. We made it to the cafe, devoured a couple of thousand calories and returned home. On the drive back I think I may have been caught by a police camera, probably for doing 32.5mph in 30mph zone. Twice in a week, not good. My dislike for these devices is growing to Jeremy Clarkson-type proportions. That's the first rant of the day over, apart from the 'Beach Dog Club' of course. The second rant is about things that you buy that break but you can't take them back as you have lost the receipt. The third is people that owe you money but avoid you like you have the Ebola virus. Don't stop me, I'm on a roll. The fourth rant of the day concerns the chavs who have abused the local playground - it's now ruined, good work there. The fifth is the madness you have to contend with when attempting to buy a few pints of milk at the supermarket as the person in front is stockpiling for a possible nuclear disaster. The sixth is something I heard second-hand that really annoyed me. A friend of mine told me he bumped into a local footballer (no names mentioned) and his wife doing some Christmas shopping. Whilst the lads were chatting, the lad's wife lent over and said 'isn't it great that the credit crunch doesn't affect the likes of us'. Someone get me a gun. To think it is bad enough, but to say it is a joke. Let's just hope she trips up on her Jimmy Choos, knocks herself out with her Gucci handbag and wakes up smelling the roses and joining in with the real world. The seventh rant of the day is about slow drivers (you know the ones, when you're in a rush they are feeding the wheel and indicating round a bend), and the eighth and final rant goes to people who... moan a lot! Ignore all of the above, life is good!

Beach Babes

Maybe it's a northern thing that my children have inherited the love of beaches and paddling in the water in winter. We drove to Blackpool Sands today, amongst other places, and within 10 minutes all three kids were waist deep in the drink. It started off gently enough with the three of them running in and out, avoiding the incoming tide, but as soon as one got wet they all decided it was a good idea to take a few layers off and wade in. It definitely raised a few eyebrows with other well wrapped-up beachgoers as my lot steamed in regardless of the sub-zero temperatures. When they eventually got cold (it took about 30 minutes) we headed off home with the heaters on full belt. Must get another in-car DVD player at some point because without some serious help, entertainment-wise, there is only so long you can withstand the screaming, fighting and laughing in the back of the car. I did smile though when we were all trying to guess Isabella's eye-spy question of 'I spy something beginning with C'. After loads of tries we gave up and asked Issy to tell us. And her answer? 'Christmas!' By the way, I have just returned from meeting Hilly (Kevin Hill). His manager at Dorchester Town wanted to get hold of the DVD of our recent game against Bath as they play them soon in the league. We had a good chat about football and work etc, as Hilly now gets dirty twice for a living - playing football and working for his brother fabricating metals. What a top lad Hilly is. He is enjoying his football and his new home and is looking forward to getting married (and the stag do!). True to form, he didn't stop bouncing the whole time we were talking. See you Sunday mate.

TUESDAY, 23 DECEMBER 2008

Final preps

I'm currently knee deep in pressies and flat-pack items, so uber-quick blog tonight. Myself, Steve Woods, Lee Mansell and Chris Todd went to Torbay

Hospital this afternoon to drop a few presents off and to see some of the patients in the children's ward. There really are some great people who work in that ward helping not only the children but their parents too. Quite a few of the guys we met today will be spending Christmas in hospital, which must be extremely difficult for both them and their families. I hope that the New Year brings health and happiness for them. At least we made one young lad's day with our visit. He had a Liverpool top on, and so on receiving his gifts he was delighted to get a Torquay autograph book so that he could get the signatures of his favourite Liverpool players!

Merry Christmas

To all readers of the blog, TUFC supporters, family and friends: I hope that you have a great Christmas. Hope to see some of you on Boxing Day at Weymouth, or if you have had too many Quality Streets or need some fresh air, feel free to pop down to the racecourse tomorrow morning to watch training, K.O. 9.30am. Thanks so much to all who have read the blog, I hope you have enjoyed reading it as much as I have enjoyed writing it. The Herald Express asking me to start the blog was a real bonus and I am really grateful for their support, namely Andy, Guy and Dave. I must also say Happy Christmas and a massive thanks to all the staff at the club, especially Kerry, Sally and Ann, who always go out of their way to help myself (a lot!), the lads and our families on match days. My children are buzzing with excitement - it will be great to see their faces light up (early) on Xmas morning. Let's hope Santa has been generous. My wish list is the same as usual: lots of points, a Chocolate Orange and a nice bottle of red.

Merry Christmas,
Love, health and happiness to all.

P.S. Regarding recent comments about dogs - I love them really, especially Bella and Jake (The Mansells' pooches).

FRIDAY, 26 DECEMBER 2008

Home and Away games

A good victory, a bad game and a fantastic following. That about sums up today's match *(won 1-0 at Weymouth)*. Hope those who travelled to Weymouth have now thawed out and are tucking into some nice turkey sandwiches. Lets move on now to Sunday for more points and the last of the turkey. It will be a quick training session in the morning and then it's back home to relax and crack on with Lego building, Wii playing and farmyard constructing. Bring it on.

SUNDAY, 28 DECEMBER 2008

Gutted

Gutted is an understatement about today's result *(lost 1-0 to Kidderminster)*. Losing at home against a team that had one shot on target in 90 minutes is hard to take. We have been punished for not taking our chances in a big way. The performance was very similar to that against Histon at home last week and we won that 4-1. But if you don't take your chances, and we didn't this afternoon, this game that drives us all mad has a habit of hurting you. The Kidderminster players and their 40 fans celebrated at the final whistle like they had won the league, and I'm not surprised as they should have been beaten by four or five. As a player, you have to take it on the chin but I can tell you that losing a game like that is a real killer. I'm that angry I feel like wrecking the place and throwing my boots through the window, but I don't think that would go down too well with my wife and kids. Having my family at games is great, but trying to remain calm after losses is difficult. My boy takes it really badly - in fact he kicked the seat in front so hard he thinks he may have broken his foot. I could go on all night and probably will to myself when everyone is in bed, but the fact is it's done. If anyone thinks that as a player you leave the ground after a match and turn off, you couldn't be further from the truth. All the lads will be extremely low until the next training session and the next win. For now I will be putting on a brave face and getting on with family life whilst suffering from a massive case of internal combustion. Thank you as ever for your support.

MONDAY, 29 DECEMBER 2008

Eden

I woke up still in one heck of a bad mood today, but spurred on by the family, took a trip out to the Eden Project. It is something that we have always thought would be good to do but have never got round to doing. What surprised me about Eden was that the first major steps to creating this amazing place started in 1998, the year Cameron, our son, was born in Plymouth. It has taken that long to visit. If you haven't yet been, I will try not to ruin it for you, but let's get a few facts out of the way first. Ten years ago, the Eden site was a used-up China Clay pit. It has been transformed into a global garden housed in huge biomes (one of which is the biggest greenhouse in the world). The Eden Project includes landscapes, crops and wild plants as well as its own rain forest. It definitely makes you think about the environment and the stresses that we exert on our planet. The best stats of the day were those of the 'seed'. Given its own mammoth display cabinet, this huge copy of a seed was carved from one piece of rock weighing in at 167 tonnes (the biggest single piece of rock ever excavated). Eventually coming in at 70 tonnes after completion, it was lifted into place in a spanking new building, much to the relief, I'm sure, of the man who spent most of the 10,000 hours needed to carve it. Stats over. All in all a good day out.

An extra bonus tonight as my bro Mark and his son Harvey have rolled into town for a few days. It will be great to catch up and have a few shandies. I may even look over some of the books he has brought with him, one of which I have just seen titled 'Equity and Trusts' (he is currently taking a law degree). Containing around 5,000 pages, I should have that one polished off by Thursday!

Credit Crunched

What a sad sight it is at the moment seeing Woolworths shops closing around the country. I bought my first record (vinyl) from Woollies all those years ago. It has, for lots of people, after countless shopping trips, been the final destination. I'm one of those people, in recent years being dragged in to buy gifts for someone, in past years being dragged in to get my new school uniform and pencil case. A high street institution for many, I'm sure. Well, it's a goner - 200 branches going this week with the rest of the 600 due to close before January 5. I'm sure Frank Woolworth will be turning in his grave to see the brand come to an end. He was the man who, while running his multi-million dollar chain of 5 and 10 cents stores, decided it was time to go big. In 1913 he gave the go-ahead and the money ($13.5million paid in cash) for the construction of the world's tallest skyscraper, the Woolworth Building, to be built in New York. On completion it rose to 55 floors, achieving his goal of it being the biggest building and with it gaining some serious bragging rights. The brand had started. The neo-Gothical beast of a building obviously still stands in 2008, proudly sitting between newer but no less impressive structures. But poor old Woollies and its 30,000 employees does not. Yes, I have given you facts. Yes, I have given you heartache - but at least one person was happy. My wife nipped in today for a few last-minute bargains while I was being used for target practice at the bombing site (four kids and me at the swimming pool). By the way, I saw David James out shopping today. I bumped into

79

him in Office while looking at a pair of trainers. And what thought popped into my head? Does he look at a pair of runners and say to himself 'do I really need these trainers and when is it pay day?' Not wanting to pry, I answered the question myself – 'get a grip pal, I'm living the dream. I'll have two pairs in white and two in black and I don't care when it's pay day baby, I'm a multi...' I walked out empty-handed, it's a five-week month! Still, we will both be playing in the same cup competition this weekend. You can't buy that.

WEDNESDAY, 31 DECEMBER 2008

New Year's Eve

Tonight, for millions of people, will involve lots of alcohol, maybe some food, most definitely a conga, and without doubt a few half-hearted but well-intentioned New Year's resolutions. You know the ones - stop smoking, stop gambling, no more chocolate, save more money, stop swearing, work harder, no more dressing up as a woman (men), and even no more New Year's resolutions. I will take on board the last two (I mean one, of course) of these examples. For me, the last 15 or so New Year's Eves have been spent at home with family or friends bringing in the New Year quietly. The reason being, of course, football. Playing on New Year's Day is hard enough anyway, but hungover is not great. Saying that, back in the day, whilst playing for Grimsby, I remember going out partying one New Year's Eve. It started with a few social drinks and ended with me throwing a few shapes in Pier 39 (Cleethorpes' premier nightclub) and throwing a few punches outside Pier 39 (Cleethorpes' premier nightclub). Oh, and I nearly fell out of a window that night. You may be thinking how did the game go? The answer is very well. We beat Fulham 4-3 and I happened to smash one into the top corner. I wouldn't recommend it though. Looking back it seems crazy, especially considering how disciplined you have to be now to stay in the game. If you have guidance, discipline and a portion of luck early on in your career it gives you a great chance of success. However, if any or all of those traits are absent then it can be trouble. As they say, hindsight is a wonderful thing. I know one thing for sure - I am more than happy to be watching 'Chitty Chitty Bang Bang' with my babes this afternoon, having a nice meal later on and seeing in the New Year at home rather than celebrating it by 'high-fiving' someone I don't know in a club listening to 'Come on Eileen'. Hold on though! No game tomorrow... let's party! Only joking - Happy New Year to one and all from all at Hargreaves Towers.

Bring on 2009!!!

Whether you were out partying, in partying or not partying at all, I hope all readers had a great New Year's Eve. We watched a bit of Jools Holland last night, as always great talent on show including the Ting Tings, Adele, Lily Allen, Sam Sparrow, Duffy and Annie Lennox to name but a few. The audience looked like they were having a great night, as did a host of celebs watching on with Al Murray, Gav (from Gavin and Stacey), a well-lubricated Lennie Henry and lots of actors and singers alike all enjoying the show. I am determined to be in that audience next year so I'd better start now because it will take some serious blagging. I got quite a few texts last night with some great videos of bad singing, dancing and falling over to keep as reminders. My efforts at New Year's resolutions are broken already. Not swearing (head tennis today), not spending (bought shoes today) and not drinking (medicinal glass of red with dinner) are all easier said than done. Looking back at last year, on and off the field, was interesting. Play-offs, a cup final and player-of-the-year awards, a real rollercoaster of emotions. Off the field, four house moves, a few family tragedies and of course Toddy's news meant much of the same. Just a normal year really! Oh, and I forgot to mention the culling of cars and credit cards in honour of the credit crunch. As well as today being the beginning of a New Year, it also brings a change of mood. It has taken me five days to shake off last Saturday's loss but now the cloud has lifted, a third round tie in the FA Cup will do nicely. Here's hoping for a successful, healthy and prosperous New Year for all.

F.A Cup 4th Round Draw

Time: 2.05pm. Q. Who will it be?
Time: 4.45pm. A. Coventry City at home.
Just returned from the club after watching the fourth round draw. With so many Premiership clubs going in the first few ties, our chances of getting a big club were dwindling fast. Seeing us get Coventry was at first a bit of a blow, but although it could have been better it could certainly have been a lot worse. The club will make money, we are playing a Championship club and it is a game that we can win! See you on the 24th.

I must just mention yesterday's game *(won 1-0, Blackpool at home, FA Cup third round).* The lads put so much effort into that performance and thoroughly deserved to win. There was a great feeling in the changing room before the match, never mind after. The atmosphere in the stands was also great, it really helps the team to see and hear the fans out in force. I, along with quite a few of my team-mates, feel a bit battered and bruised today. After some games it can really feel like you have hardly broken sweat (usually games that have been won) whereas after others it can feel like you have been involved in a prize-fight, which brings me nicely onto my late-night TV exploits. When all was quiet, my parents had retired as had my wife and children, I started to trawl the channels and there it was – 'The Thriller in Manila'. All I can say is if you haven't seen it, then watch it. Two of the world's best heavyweights, Muhammad Ali and Joe Frazier, fight head-to-head in Manila for 14 gruelling rounds. In the end, the Frazier corner stop their fighter from taking part in the 15th round as they feared for his life. He had fought almost the entire 14th round blind, such was the damage to his eyes. This resulted in Ali winning the fight. Unbeknown to the Frazier corner, Ali after the 14th round had sat down on his stool completely shattered and said 'cut my gloves off, I'm done. It's over'. This would have handed Frazier victory but as it transpired, they had already made the decision and Ali's victory it was. To this day, Frazier still shows a real hate for Ali who in the lead up to the fight had made a few personal comments about him. In 2008, Ali apologised, but over 30 years on and Joe Frazier is unrepentant. His answerphone message says it all. 'My name is Joe Frazier, sharp as a razor. Yeah, floats like a butterfly, stings like a bee (Ali's famous boast). I'm the man who done the job. He knows, look and see. Call me, bye bye'. Which basically means 'look at Muhammad Ali now, suffering badly from Parkinson's Syndrome - I did that to him'. Pretty hardcore stuff. An amazing fight, an amazing programme.

MONDAY, 5 JANUARY 2009

Busy doing nothing

A quick visit to the hospital this morning for an MOT and then it was supposed to be a day at home resting. Unfortunately on my return I walked straight into trouble. A combination of an early spring clean and the dismantling of the Christmas decorations put paid to any chances of watching 'This Morning' or putting a tube of Chocolate Hob Nobs through the dunking test. Finally, after several trips to Argos (for storage devices) and Tesco (the cattle market, miscellaneous) the clean-up operation was over. It took 10 hours. The mood in the house is tense this evening as tomorrow signals the return for the children to school. Fiona, my wife, however is ecstatic! Big game tomorrow so need rest, hence TTFN.

Game Off

Sorry it's a slightly later blog tonight. Obviously we have no game this evening, which I think is a good thing. A time to rest and enjoy last Saturday will do the team and our supporters the world of good. I was able to take the children to athletics tonight, sub-zero conditions for those taking part and those watching (myself). Now I know what it feels like to lose all sensation in your toes like a footy fan in mid-winter. Whilst typing away I have been glancing over at the TV. My wife is watching 'Claire Sweeney - My Big Fat Diet'. Claire has just visited Ross King (TV journo) at his LA home. Set in the hills overlooking the L of A, this sprawling pad is the result of writing and talking. Bring it on baby, bring it on! Diary (my wife's) permitting, I would like to take my boy Cam to the NEC in Birmingham this weekend as the Auto Sport International is in town. Stunts, racing, demos by F1 stars and an attempt to break the 1,000 mph barrier await. Truth be told, I will probably take him for a spin to buy Top gear magazine. Lastly, I have just spotted in a magazine's gadget section that 3's INQ1 phone comes highly recommended. Set to make Britain's social-networking addiction worse than ever, this Facebook-friendly phone is a 'oner' and is on pay as you go. Well to that I say, if the signal is as bad as it is on my 3 network's excuse for a phone, then expect to be making some pretty hair-raising trips to your rooftop to make or receive a call. My daughter Harriet's phone has a better reception, and that is plastic and plays 'Fi-Fi and the Flowertots'. There are some benefits though - you will never exceed your talk time.

THURSDAY, 8 JANUARY 2009

The Captain's Wife's Blog

After weeks of being subjected to the ramblings of my husband, he thought that it would be a good idea if I was to take hold of the reigns for a special edition guest blog. So here we go - this is how it really is in the world of football and in the Hargreaves household. The truth - hot off the press from a Blue Square Premier WAG. The gloves are off now honeybun – as they say in Yorkshire, 'the truth will out'. Well it has been a long journey down to Devon and Torquay, about 20 years at the last count. You will be surprised, or not, to know that I have been beside the long-haired dynamo (gyppo as sometimes referred to on the terraces) since that first game at Grimsby Town aged 17 with short hair and even shorter shorts! Yes, I was there freezing to death trying to look glam aged 17 and wearing very unsuitable clothing. Blundell Park has got be one of the coldest grounds in the country, but I could take it back then. On a Saturday evening I could be found queueing - Christian walked straight to the front! - at Pier 39, which is, as mentioned in a previous blog, a lovely nightclub, braving storm-force gales and tidal waves, and sporting my latest velvet hot pants and bra top. It was the '80s so please forgive me. So Saturday afternoons on the terraces were not too bad in comparison. Twenty years on, I have realised that thermals and sensible shoes are essential if you are to enjoy watching the game. I have to say though, Saturday's game against Blackpool was extremely cold, but the Hargreaves family kept warm by jumping up and down frequently and shouting a lot. I am not one for sitting calmly and saying nothing at games. I'm afraid when it comes to watching number 14 Chris Hargreaves we are all quite vocal (Mrs Hargreaves, my mother-in-law, in particular!) Torquay United is truly a family-friendly club and we are all very well looked after. Many of the players and wives have children and even those who don't all get on well. We have been at many clubs (10 I think, maybe more - I've lost count) and wives, girlfriends and children are often forgotten. Not that we expected to be treated differently, but it is nice to see friendly faces on a match day. I remember one club we were at for two

seasons, the same people gave me my tickets every week and asked me my name every time for two whole years. I must have one of those faces easily forgotten. That was the same club that I walked past a certain Mrs Mansell for a whole season without either of us saying hello. We do laugh about it now, but it just goes to show how different things can be. On to the main man, Mr Hargreaves. Well, what can I say about him? Well there's a lot I can tell you - the highs, the lows and the in-between times, but I think most importantly it is that as a player he has always given 110 per cent to every club he has been at. He is dedicated to his profession and always tries to do the right things to stay fit and healthy. That is one of the reasons he is still playing today. The main reason is, of course, me. My support, my sympathetic ear after a defeat, the fact I always make sure there is ice in the freezer for all of those sore groins and that I am always so interested to hear how the games have gone. Behind every great man there is ALWAYS an even greater woman. It's so true! I think that I will leave the embarrassing stories and moans about his bad habits (shocking, but he's not perfect - he does have some) until my next guest spot. I have however managed to find a couple of pictures that I'm sure you will all appreciate. I'll sign off for now as I'm currently multi-tasking: cooking the dinner, bathing Harriet, putting her to bed, writing this blog, checking Facebook and getting the uniforms ready for school in the morning. All tasks need to be completed by 8.45pm when the remaining Hargreaves family members return from football training and athletics. The second serving of dinner will then commence, followed by more bathing children and we may get to sit down about 10ish for five minutes before bed. So you can see that it is a very glamorous life that we live.

Fiona

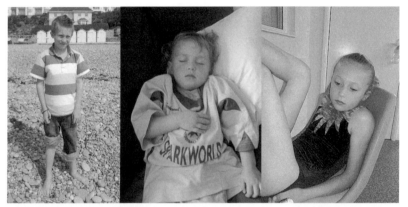

*(left to right) Cameron on the beach; Watching dad is hard work –
Harriet, known as The Beast, has a snooze; Issy the gymnast*

Issy, Cameron, Fiona and Harriet consider a bit of boating

The Next Generation – Cameron flies down the wing

The Hargreaves surf squad ready to take on the waves

(above) Arabian Nights – Me and Jase dressed up for the Moroccan cook-off; (below) Kev Nicholson enjoys our domestic bliss

(above) Damien Davey with his 'Boat-class' Mercedes; (below) Scott Bevan, 'The Bevanator'

(clockwise from top left) (below) Robbo in his going-out gear; Me in my Rick Astley phase; Emergency repairs to make sure my lucky boots see me through the last six games of the season;

Clockwise from top – Mustapha Carayol is fed wine gums on the team coach; Martin Rice trains for the Tour de France; Steve Adams, aka 'The Ghoul' – be afraid, be very afraid...

(top) Lee Hodges finds a picture of Mark Ellis; (bottom) Wayne Carlisle and Lee Mansell with some liquid refreshment

The journey home from Wembley – (top) me, the trophy and Scott Bevan, and (bottom) Chris Todd

Work Time Home Time

OK, lots to talk about, notably my wife's recent blog posting and her kind (!) addition of old pictures from the late '80s - now I know why I have kept the laptop away from her for this long. To be honest, it could have been a lot worse though. For the countless years of house moves, the location changes, the long phone calls to agents whilst on holiday every year, the uncertainty and the amount of stressful games I have subjected her to, she could have really gone to town on me. I don't think my football career has affected her in a negative way, in fact the counselling is down to two sessions a week now and the handbag fetish is tapering off to one a month. Onto football, we are all set for the FA Trophy game against Rushden tomorrow hoping for the same type of run that saw us reach Wembley last year. Training, as usual, has been competitive over the last few days. A head-high Michael Brough tackle was a real highlight - we were winning a small-sided game quite comfortably and, as is the norm, someone usually loses it on the opposing side. That person was Broughy and the recipient? Yes, moi. It was only a tickle and although Broughy, as is the norm, was very apologetic, it was already forgotten. These things happen. Saying that, vengeance did come in the form of an epic head tennis game after training that same day. The usual suspects of Hargreaves, Woods and Hodges took on the wannabes of Mansell, Nicholson and Brough. The first game, to 21, was dispatched in typical style by the old boys. Onto the next game, this one was much closer - a combination of our need for a hot bath or some decent opponents and their desire to chase the ball into the next field, suffering spinal damage (Broughy), to salvage a point. The banter is usually white hot in these games, but the sight of Kev Nicholson smashing the ball in to his own face whilst trying to retrieve a set by Manse will go down in head tennis folklore. Everyone on that court was on the floor in fits of laughter after that shot. It was that funny we had to take a short break to compose ourselves and wipe away the tears. Add to that the effort involved in the salmon-like leap made by 'Lamby' Mansell to head a ball into our court, only to see it delicately bounce off the wool on his head and provide us with a point, and we were really finding it hard to play on. Whether it was down to these incidents, the improvement of the opposition or the fact that our bodies were creaking, the old boys found themselves game point down. Was it their time to celebrate and gloat and for us to face a walk of shame? Of course not - come on, I wouldn't be writing this if that had happened. The danger was averted and a couple of minutes later victory was ours - a devastating psychological blow for our opponents who were visibly shaken. There's always next time lads. It is great to be one of last ones at training, on the pitch or in the gym. Family and body permitting, I would be out there all day. I just wish I had done it in the first few years of my career. This I tell to the younger lads all the time. Rushing home to go to the pub or to mess about was the norm for me back then, but it was a big mistake – career-wise, I strongly recommend anyone who wants to succeed to get the most out of each day rather than rush home to complete the next level on Grand Theft Auto.

SUNDAY, 11 JANUARY 2009

Weekender

The changing room was filled with laughter as usual yesterday, only this time it was at my expense. Having let my wife loose on the blog, and her subsequent posting of a few old-school (literally) pictures, it was only a matter of time before they filtered into the changing room - and yes, it was time yesterday to face the music. A picture of a young CH at school with a rascal jumper on, and another with a Rick Astley hairdo and a Simon Cowell waistline definitely kept the boys amused pre-match. Feel free to laugh out loud as they will stay posted for another 24 hours. A good result yesterday in the Trophy *(beat Rushden 1-0)* means that we are in the last 16 of the competition with our eyes now firmly set on Wembley. As it stands at the moment, the club are competing in three competitions, which is great. Financially, the more games and gate receipts the better. Obviously for the supporters it becomes expensive, so to all those who cheer us on a big thank you. We went to our friends last night for dinner and what a night it was. Currently at 1-1 in the 'celebrity chef recipe cook-offs' we were treated to a feast. The pressure was starting to build for us (Fiona) to top the meal put before us, the starter and main course were of epic standard. Only when I noticed my wife's clenched fists under the table and her sympathetic words (hidden delight) did I realise that the Gordon Ramsey dessert had under-performed/whisked. Why does everything have to be a competition? I don't know but after we next invite our friends over for dinner/victory, the next meal we have together will be either be cooked by the men or brought to the table in bags - I think Indian would be nice. Back to last night's late-night entertainment, the work-out session laid on by the birthday boy in the garden was second to none. Happy birthday Jason, and a great birthday suit!

Breaking news! My boy Cam was playing at Liverpool's academy today and he scored against the mighty Reds. A belter in the bottom corner will make the return to school tomorrow all the more bearable, especially when he demonstrates the finish to his mates. Finally, thanks to my bro Mark, who came down this weekend to watch the game with his son, Harvey. Good banter, good chats and unexpected baby-sitting duties meant for a top time.

MONDAY, 12 JANUARY 2009

TV Heartache

I watched a repeat of Channel 4's 'Surviving Gazza' last night, and I'm sure as all those who managed to catch it would agree, it made for pretty traumatic viewing. The nation's favourite, a legend, showman and entertainer, Gazza was clearly very ill. The family's attempt to help him was always going to be tough one. We all remember the heroics and tears of Italia 90 and have watched with interest as his career took him to Italy and Scotland - the move from Tottenham to Lazio and from there Glasgow

Rangers. As usual, it's the private life of Gazza that has dominated the papers, with his drinking, drug-taking and brawls hitting the headlines. But last night's documentary showed the other side of the story, his long-suffering family pouring their hearts out, especially ex-wife Sheryl, who I reckon has seen some sights over the past few decades. The children all seemed pretty well-grounded although it did look like Regan, his youngest son, had had enough of the drama. I don't blame him really, considering the upbringing he's had. You can't be totally one-sided about it but the footage of Sheryl in tears made me think she was being honest about the whole thing - heavy drinking and violence and the follow-on lack of a dad around resulted in a bad few years for the kids as well. In the programme, Gazza was allowed to spend some time back at the family home yet within a couple of weeks - of erratic behaviour - he was off. A small argument had escalated into a falling-out and he left, firstly to go on tour with Iron Maiden (bad move considering their rider has as much drink on it as Threshers has on its shelves and probably enough gear to keep Shaun Ryder happy), secondly holed up in a hotel room somewhere in Europe. So the decision was made to track him down, and when they had, the whole family travelled to Portugal to confront him. Either he tries to sort himself out or that's that. Having found him in a hotel room looking a total wreck, and after his hurls of abuse, the family decided to go home, upset but relieved. The show ended with Sheryl saying there had been no contact with Gazza in the last three months. He is now in the Second Chance clinic and is under the supervision of Peter Kay (come on, not that Peter Kay, he's not in Phoenix Nights). This Peter Kay is the man who has tried, with some success, to sort out a number of high-profile footballers. He was the man who recently chaperoned Joey Barton on his release from jail. I came across him while on my UEFA B course a few seasons back. He gave a speech about drink and drugs in football and the help that is now on offer to players (I still say on offer to all top, well-known, well-off players, but the truth is Joe Bloggs on peanuts in the lower leagues may not be so lucky, and if he's not it's game over). On that same UEFA B course and during that same speech, Paul Davis, ex-Arsenal and England player and now an assessor on the courses, mentioned to Peter Kay that he had a friend who needed help quite badly. Peter Kay's answer was, as he tells all, 'tell him to ring me if he really wants to help himself'. I recently saw a comment in a newspaper from Mr Kay referring to Gazza's situation, saying 'I have been waiting for that call for six years'. I didn't realise at the time that Paul Davis was talking about Gazza. Let's hope this rehab, maybe his last chance, does the trick. I asked my wife her opinion and she said of Gazza 'complete loser, had everything, not strong enough'. Wow, don't mess eh! I think great player and national institution but the drink has made him in to a bad dad which is, as I have seen with friends of mine, the final straw. I also used to see a physio friend of mine while I was at Northampton called John Sheridan. He was the Tottenham physio when Gazza was there and aided his recovery from injury and subsequent move to Lazio. He always said 'he is one in a million, a real diamond'. Only time will tell if he becomes one again.

TUESDAY, 13 JANUARY 2009

Bullet

Quick posting tonight due to extreme lack of time. Therefore I will give you today's events in bullet-point form.

1. Harriet jumped on us both at 5.20am.
2. I eventually broke about 6.30am and accepted defeat (with that came five lots of Fifi and the Flowertots, a bottle of milk and peanut butter on toast (not for me)
3. Kids dispatched to school
4. Training started at 10.30am. At around 11.15am I was on the receiving end of a magnificent sliding tackle, and the player responsible? Danny Stevens. Don't mess with Dan when he is angry otherwise the Cockney warrior will destroy.
3b. Big moment for the head tennis wannabes. The score was tied, was it

finally going to be glory for the pretenders? No, Woodsy had to be in Paignton for 1pm! Unlucky lads.

4b. Bevanator, Toddy and myself did a core/weights session after training (summer is coming after all)

5. Eventually got home about 5.20pm after meeting up with Guy at the Herald Express.

6. Cooked bangers and mash as Fiona was under a biblical pile of ironing.

7. Going out soon to meet a friend so it's more Fifi then Hatty's bedtime. Cam and Issy back shortly from athletics.

8. May blog again later as I still have to erase the picture of me at school with my Christmas jumper on.

9. See ya!

9b. Sorry for any grammatical errors, will sort later.

WEDNESDAY, 14 JANUARY 2009

Return of the Todd

The Setanta cameras were in today to film Chris Todd's comeback. Also present were the BBC, ITV, Channel 4 and CNN, as well as representatives from Men's Health, Vogue, Horse and Hounds, Homes and Gardens and The Beano.

OK, maybe I have over-egged the pudding a bit but you get the message. A rapid-fire return for Toddy, it seems remarkable that in such a short time he has made such massive progress. This could be down to several reasons. Our crack physio Damien Davey - not his treatment but his high-quality banter. They say laughter is the best medicine.

The air quality on the coast - years ago if you were ill, it was off to the seaside for a stick of rock and some deep breathing.

Or could it be a one-a-day tablet and a big portion of will power. Let's call it a combination of all four.

Training was also filmed with a few of the lads finding some bobbles and shin touches.

One man was certainly up for it today. Martin 'Get on Mart' Rice was throwing himself everywhere, pulling off some Banks-like saves. Well done Mart, but I think trying to get a copy for all the family is milking it a bit! He was that pleased he nipped over to Tesco and bought a couple of steaks for tea to celebrate... beware Becky, beware!

After training, head tennis and weights (yes weights, yes core, yes European beach ban may be imposed) I headed for the showers where again I enjoyed/suffered an ice-cold shower. This is not for fitness reason. Tyrone, Muzzi, Nicky Wroe, Robbo and Danny Stevens are under suspicion of using up all the hot water by cleaning their boots in the showers. Added to that, Mark Ellis literally washes his skin away, he spends that long in there. The same can't be said for Elliot, who only showers for 12 seconds. He is like a cat, dislikes water but likes licking himself. Referring back to head tennis and after another heavy defeat and some serious in-fighting, Lee Mansell and Michael Brough are looking for a new member, and their requirements? Must have a positive mentality. Must like fun. Must like chocolate. Must not wear woolly jumpers and Timberlands at 8am. I think they are being extremely harsh Kev, you will soon be back in the circle of trust.

THURSDAY, 15 JANUARY 2009

Supper Time

Tomorrow we face Wrexham. It will be a tough game but they all are, so there's nothing new in that. As usual, we are looking to gain three points and hopefully start to hunt down Burton. I have been hammering it a bit in training this week and with that in mind I bid you farewell as I have a date with some good friends of mine. Voltarol, crushed ice and high-strength Multi-Vit are joining me for a spot of supper. Bon appétit.

Moody Blues

Well what can I say? Only that I've been in an extremely bad mood today and it's not lifting. After 19 years I still can't get my head around defeats, or draws that seem like defeats *(drew 1-1 with Wrexham)*. The performance wasn't great but we still should have won. What can we do? Nothing - just get back on the training ground on Monday and look forward to a great game on Saturday. With that in mind, I should have shaken my mood by about Wednesday. Until then the wife and kids will be in hiding (only joking).

Quote of the Day

I was reading The Observer the other day (as you do) and in the sport section David Hills, the sports writer, gave a great insight into today's ruthless game in the form of some wild quotes by players, managers and chairman alike. Here are a few of my favourites.

James Beattie, November 2008, furious at reports that he may leave Sheffield Utd in January: 'My long-term future is here - I'd be happy to finish my career at United. I came here to do a job, to get us back in the top flight. Why would I want to leave for another club? I've never been happier anywhere.' On joining Stoke this January: 'I'm delighted'. I'm sure you are... ker-ching!

Craig Bellamy, December 2008: 'It's that time of year again- there's always a lot of speculation about people going in the transfer window. But I'm very happy at West Ham - I'm never going to go in and ask for a move.' 16 Jan: Goes in and asks for a move.

Real Madrid chief **Ramon Calderon**, January 14: 'We were all unpleasantly surprised to read the allegations made by the newspaper (Marca). The media must stop publishing lies. I've put a lot of effort into this job. Why should I resign? It's not in my character to resign, and it would not help my team. It would be irresponsible.' Two days later, Jan 16, he resigns. 48 hours is a long time in football.

It's a funny old game, yes it's hilarious in fact. Brazilian club Gremio have sanctioned a new policy of giving their players Viagra before high-altitude Copa Libertadores games. Known to give improved oxygenation to the blood, they reckon it will give the boys a real edge to their performances. They could be right, and apparently all players' wives and girlfriends have fully endorsed the product.

NB: I am currently waiting for an email from Kevin Nicholson. Titled 'My Side of the Story' it is a chance for him to get his own back on me for the months of abuse I have subjected him to - fairly of course . Watch this space for said blog, once it has been given the once-over and fully edited by yours truly.

TUESDAY, 20 JANUARY 2009

Kevin Nicholson - 'My Story' (uncensored)

I'm going to enjoy this and I want the un-edited version to be shown. Can I just say that it is an honour and a pleasure to be invited to write on such a stage as the 'Captain's Blog'. First things first, Chris Hargreaves is a great man. If he is editing this he may just leave it there but I hope he allows me my say. He is a talented footballer with exceptional levels of fitness and determination, he has a will to win which is rivalled only by a select few greats of the game and a physique which makes you forget that he is nearing 50 and has been in the game of football for at least three decades. He is a moderately attractive man who has worked hard with the hand God has dealt him. He dresses well, although it must be tiring trying to find adult-looking t-shirts in Baby Gap, and his shiny gypsy-like hair stands him apart from most men. He snagged the gorgeous Fiona at school so she can't be blamed for settling for him as she was young and was not given a fighting chance of spreading her wings and ending up with some one more in her league. This said, between them they have brought into the world three great kids who could probably get by on their looks alone but have all been gifted with talents of their own and personalities to go with it. I am expecting big things from them all. Greavsie dotes on his family and his love for them is overshadowed only by his love for himself, and on this note I will begin my side of the story. He has taken great delight trying to tarnish my good name on this blog, painting a picture of me as a paranoid, OCD-suffering hater of all things, but this is his true talent. They say you can take a horse to water but you can't make it drink... well Greavsie could. If he was a defence lawyer he would have a backlog of criminals holding smoking guns safe in the knowledge that Torquay Utd's number 14 will talk any judge round and get them off scot-free. He is the master of manipulation, the world's greatest blag artist. My first dealings with Tarzan were many years ago at Northampton Town, where he was a legend. However, in my time there he didn't say a word to me, preferring to ignore the young lad and focus on his love for Vivienne Westwood jackets. We met up again at the start of last season and ended up living in Toddy's old house. This is where I first learned of his ability to change his mind and opinion at record speed, and how he could hypnotise me into taking him house-hunting in the middle of pre-season while my legs were ready to drop off. He talks about my love of showers but fails to mention his love at taking all his clothes off at random times of the day and doing press-ups in the kitchen through fear of father time catching up with him. The first time he met my fiancé, Jenny, he was sat topless doing his beloved 'pec dance' and he immediately turned her on me, which resulted in me not being able to shower for a week without third-degree burns while they sat downstairs turning the cold water on and off, laughing at my high-pitched screams of frustration. In the early days of this blog he talked about the pub quiz we had on the way to an away game and how he led his team to a glorious victory. He was actually on my team and I sat with a pen and paper next to him while he confidently looked me the eye and gave me the 'correct' answers, of which about 75 per cent were wrong, at no point listening to me or Wayne Carlisle's desperate attempts to contribute and stave off an embarrassing defeat. In training we do possession circles where the aim of the game is to keep the ball away from the two chasing players in the middle of the circle with one and two-touch passes. The person who gives the ball away then takes over in the middle. Unless you are Hargreaves, in which case you pass the ball to the players in the middle then look at the person next to you, whose eyes then glaze over, and he awakens in the middle of the circle alongside another hapless victim chasing the ball and wondering what has just happened. Finally... HEAD TENNIS! Hargreaves, Woods, Hodges versus Brough, Nicholson, Mansell. Every week the same happens. CH stands in a corner next to the net, his partners run around and feed him the ball, he chests the ball over the net, shouts 'TRADEMARK' at the top of his voice then runs around screaming and laughing like a five-year-old whether he scores a point or not. The rally continues until he decides he has had enough, at which point he generally catches the ball and, with his two ageing groupies stood behind him, cheats us out of another hard-earned point with more talk and mind games. The next I see of it is when he has rushed home and told the kids how daddy pulled his team back from the brink and posts more lies on this blog. One day we will out-and-out destroy the three old amigos and he will be forced to admit defeat on this blog, but until then I can only hope that you have read this and had an insight into the real Chris Hargreaves, and that he may apologise to me for the slander that has been thrown my way on this blog. Probably not though. Love you Tarzan, xxx

Kevin Nicholson

Gutted

Lost *(1-0 at home to Coventry City)*. Set piece, 87th minute. Game over. Oh, and a broken nose after 20 minutes. Thanks for your fantastic support, what an atmosphere today. I should be writing this whilst looking forward to the fifth round draw but as we all know this game has a nasty habit of kicking you in the ********.

Blues Over

Back to work tomorrow as millions are, just in different circumstances. We will train in the morning then travel to Brighton where we are staying before the Lewes game. Then it's back to business, a case of picking up valuable points in the league. I will have to stop typing now as my wife is watching 'Box-Aerobics' in the background - not working out, just watching whilst quaffing white wine. Surely there is more on TV than that. Back in Devon Wednesday 0300 hours. Speak again then.

It's the wife again!

Hi, apologies for not taking to the laptop last night, I just simply ran out of time and energy. I had agreed to do the blog in the absence of CH, as the lads travelled to Brighton ahead of their game this evening. The boys will be away a lot this week and to be honest it gives me a welcome break from football. I did not make the game at the weekend as Isabella had a throat infection. I didn't mind, I have been to many of these 'big' games before and although we were not there in body to support dad, he knows how much we think of him and that he will give it everything. So the girls stayed at home and relaxed. Mama Mia and Camp Rock were on the menu, and what a lovely afternoon we had. It's a strange time at the moment and I've gone into survival mode. We are having a good season, although sometimes it may not feel like it, and I think that some people forget that. The lads are under a lot of pressure to perform and it does tend to come home with them. Unfortunately there is no escape. Everyone wants to talk to you about it, from the school gate and the supermarket to the queue for loo in M&S! I don't mind as people are always complimentary, and of course it's his job and with that comes certain responsibilities. However at the moment with the end of the season in sight and our future a little uncertain I will enjoy taking a step away from football banter this week and concentrate on the children. Who knows what the future may hold so I will do my thing, get head around it and prepare for every eventuality. I won't be listening to the game, or watching the scores coming in on Setanta - that's just too painful. Plus I have to make a Roman Gladiator costume for Cameron by tomorrow. I will wait for the phone call.

Bye for now and good luck for tonight boys.

Fiona

WEDNESDAY, 28 JANUARY 2009

Long Way Round

I eventually stumbled into the house this morning at 4am after one heck of a journey back from Lewes. First and foremost, obviously we won and won well *(2-0)*. We needed a victory and a great team effort ensured that we got it. What a great sight it was to be playing towards our fans in both halves - incredible to see so many turn up and give the place some atmosphere. Having to stay overnight for away games means it can be a long drawn-out process, so entertainment levels can become desperate. The last time we stayed in Brighton, as blog readers will know, ended up with some of the team having a 'refreshing' dip in the sea - we all agreed that a return fixture was unnecessary, this time deciding that a relaxing stroll on Brighton Pier would be more sensible. Saying that, we nearly lost Stevie 'Ghoul' Adams, who nipped to see his mates in the Ghost Train, only surfacing when some people complained that he was too realistic - a cheap dig mate, I know, but anyway well played last night on your return and also what a great 'roomy', although the nakedness straight away was a bit of a shocker, even for my high naturist standards. The night before the game, a few of the lads, encouraged by 'Barry Norman' himself Kevin Nicholson, decided to go to the cinema to watch 'The Wrestler'. The title didn't bode well so myself and Stevie Adams ducked out and gave Brighton's livelier areas a once-over instead. Woods, Mansell, Sills and a reluctant Nicholson admitted that the £12 for the entrance fee and the pick and mix was money not well spent. I've told you, Kev, not to take onboard reviews from 'Electric Showers Weekly'. Another interesting incident on the pier involved Elliot Benyon our den-loving aardvark-fan striker. About halfway down the pier we looked down to the sea, about a 50ft drop, and discussed how long it would take, after jumping in, to swim back to shore. We reckoned about 25 minutes. Elliot suggested he would do it for £100. Knowing that the drop alone could result in major injury as well as the fact that the current was very strong, it was amazing to see how many of the lads were offering Elliot the money to jump - I think there is a strong message in there somewhere! Another first was seeing the Bevonator stand next to a height chart for a ride and be too tall for it! So with the game done and dusted it was time for the journey home. A heavy blow to both knees just before the final whistle ensured that I was in pain all the way back. Ice packs to both knees and a dicky tummy doesn't mix well. A lot of the lads get bad stomach ache after games, a combination of nervous energy, caffeine, pain-killers and pain. It can be a pretty volatile mix. Last night's winner on that front was Chris Robertson, our 'never been Scottish' centre half. The toilet area had to be roped off for Health and Safety reasons. The rest of the lads were as follows:

Mark Ellis was keeping (or not) his mate and our driver Dave (whose banter is late '70s, minimum) awake. Dave chose a quick route back, mountainous and bumpy. Wayne Carlisle also had stomach turmoil. Rosco and Matt Green were asleep. Tyrone was talking to himself. Steve Woods and Lee Mansell were watching a war DVD, officially out of the circle. Muzzi was 'Facebooking' whilst laughing on his mobile for four hours. Scott Bevan was doing press-ups and pull-ups at 12 o'clock. Danny and Elliot were giggling away at the back of the coach, playing Pro-Evo and mixing potions. Kev Nicholson was staring into his phone hoping for a call (he didn't get one) and desperately missing his quiz mate, Tim Sills, who had gone home with Mrs Sills. And Chris Hargreaves was semi-naked with knee and stomach trauma whilst watching the combined deaths of around 2,000 people (Braveheart and Band of Brothers on view). Must not forget the Ghoul, who travelled back with Damien. Damo was struggling to stay awake until the Ghoul screamed at him to avoid a speed camera. This resulted in Damo spilling and then sitting in ice cold coke for most of the journey, although he did say this morning that Stevie's presence alone was keeping him awake. So I crawled into bed at 4am feeling sick and not able to roll over. Harriet came into bed at 6.30am and so here we are. Was it all worth it? Of course it was, we got three points!

THURSDAY, 29 JANUARY 2009

Home Alone-ish

All quiet tonight, my wife has taken Cam and Issy to football and athletics respectively while she in turn puts in a last blast at step aerobics before Toddy's wedding on Sunday - why is it women never eat leading up to big events, get stressed out because their outfits aren't right and then moan that they haven't had enough time to prepare? Or is it just me? I am therefore just left with the task of entertaining, feeding and then putting to bed our little firecracker Hatty - easier said than done. Whilst doing that I am trying to fill out a tax return, which is winding me up big time. I phoned our friendly comrades at the Inland Revenue the other day and found myself on hold for 10 minutes. Unbelievably, while on hold I had to listen to a sub-standard version of the song my wife and I walked down the aisle to. All the same it did bring back memories of that day - glorious weather, great friends and all our families present made for a fantastic wedding day. It was incredible, the castle, the string quartet, the sumptuous food, in fact had I have found the right bride it would have been perfect - I'm obviously joking! The combination of incredible heat on that sunny day in June and an obscene amount of Champagne meant that some guests struggled to last the course, but isn't that what a good wedding is all about? If someone doesn't fall over the back of an antique chaise longue (Catrina), miss the first course (Auntie Margaret) or throw shapes on the dance floor like MC Hammer (Chatty) it's a bit of a bad job. Watch this space for a rundown on casualties at Toddy's wedding.

Back on the road tomorrow as we travel up to Southport. I can't wait to reacquaint myself with my concrete seat and to witness Dave our driver crank up his traffic finder.

No let-up in requirements, we would all like to go to Wembley again, hence victory is needed.

SATURDAY, 31 JANUARY 2009

Shocked

I have just returned home after the Southport game and am still in shock. All I can say is that it wasn't good enough today *(lost 1-0)*. Apologies for all those who travelled to see that performance. We are in at 9am tomorrow morning for training and have now got to forget cup competitions and return to winning ways in the league on Tuesday. Promotion can still be had and is our only thought.

But tomorrow will not be all about football, it will be about a young man who has shown tremendous character and strength and a great girl who will soon be Mrs Todd. Chris and Gemma, see you tomorrow.

Mr and Mrs Todd

We have just managed to create a snowman. It was touch and go towards the end as the snowfall had stopped, but the last remnants of snow on the roofs of cars helped us to finish it off. Freddie is now proudly sat at the front of the house with his Torquay Utd scarf and hat keeping him warm. Sledging will have to wait, risk of injury (Northampton 2002), lack of snow and lack of light mean that for now the Hargreaves bobsleigh team are out of action.

The Main event: All dressed in white, a few last-minute highlights to the hair and, oh, throw in a spray tan as well. Yes, Chris Todd was ready for the big day. After lots of handshakes and kisses, all the guests finally assembled, the groom waited for the bride to arrive. She didn't, she came to her senses just in time and unfortunately everyone was asked to leave. I'm joking of course, the music started and Gemma, looking beautiful, walked into the room. She was crying. At first we thought it was because the first person she saw in the room was Mark Ellis. But no, they were tears of joy as she made her way towards the groom, who stayed strong... just! The vows were taken, 'do you Chris Todd promise to love and cherish Gemma? Do you promise to release your credit card and accept it's a 'no' when the lads ask you to go to the local for a drink?'... 'I do'.

'Do you Gemma accept that Chris will now slacken up around the house and forget your anniversary?'... 'I do'.

'Then you are now man and wife, let the games begin'.

Soon all the guests were sat down, ready to tuck into the sumptuous meal. The seating plan at our table had been slightly adjusted - I swapped the names around so that Elliot Benyon and his lovely, long-suffering (but sane) girlfriend Kylie were not on our table. The fact that our children were present meant that Elliot may have scared our daughter Harriet too much. Saying that, the subtle swap meant that Tyrone and Muzzi were sat at our table experiencing at first hand the madness of our three children, one being the infamous Beast. Sorry about that lads. As well as Nicky Wroe and his (again) lovely girlfriend Natalie, we had the pleasure of an old mate's company. Matt 'if anyone signs in my position they're going down' Hockley and his lovely (yes there's a theme here) girlfriend Vicky made up the table. It was great to catch up with 'Hockers'. We had a good laugh chatting about football and it was interesting to hear Vicky - also a footy player, and also a midfielder - explain that she was the better player. Let me know how the one-on-ones are going, Hocks. So the speeches started, eight in total, starting with Chris – 'It's been an emotional day, even the cake is in tears'. Toddy had begun! The bride's father Brian and the groom's father Steve then had a 'speech off', both doing a top job of welcoming in new family members. The Todd brothers gave theirs, short and sweet but very funny all the same, then it was time for the best man and compere Barry. He had a longer delivery than our local postman but to be fair it had been an hour since the speeches began so his audience wanted blood. Barry did well though, after all with Toddy the material you can use about him is endless! Finally 'Bamper' Todd closed proceedings with a brilliant poem. Great stuff. The meal and subsequent banter really was tremendous. The sight of a very hot Kevin Nicholson wiping out a waitress due to his overheating gave everyone a good laugh. The fact that his jacket ended up swimming in gravy was an added bonus! Again, sorry mate. Once the meal was done it was time to catch up with old mates (well, I'd been with most of the lads in the morning but you know what I mean). Kenny Veysey was still trying to tell me a story today, Damo's setting up the scene for the joke was that long that Kenny grew a beard waiting. There was a great cameo played at night by Pete Morgan, who came over straight from the crucible (Jimmy White... 68!). The buffet was nice and came in handy later on as Elliot did some apple bobbing in the fruit salad bowl. A bit of dancing and karaoke and the day was done – well, maybe not for a couple of people! Must mention a pair

of white shoes on show, whoever wore them was either brave or mad...
thanks, yes I would say I was brave!

To Chris and Gemma.

Frozen out

Game off. Very frustrating as we wanted a victory tonight to close the gap
on the leaders. We will now have to wait until Saturday to hopefully gain
more precious points. I have just returned from taking the children to
athletics. Whilst watching the clan run, jump and throw I flicked through
today's paper. The sports pages included a list of transfers completed before
the January deadline closed. It also included a few comments from players
about their worries over contract talks. My favourite was Jimmy 'I'm a
cheeky Cockney barrow boy' Bullard, bemoaning his 'forced' transfer from
Fulham to Hull. 'I had 16 months left on my contract, and I wasn't willing
to play. I felt I needed more backing from the club'. I know, it must be so
hard for you! Poor little lamb, at least you can cheer yourself up with the
£45,000 a week you are going to get from Hull for the next four-and-a-half
years. Good luck to Toddy and Broughy, who have signed a month's loan at
Salisbury. With Histon, Crawley and Wrexham in that month's fixtures,
let's hope the boys can do us a favour!

Foreign Soil

Shattered! 9.30pm and I have just sat down, so it's a quick dip (bath,
unfortunately not indoor pool), a bite to eat and bed. I will also catch the
last half-hour of the Liverpool-Everton game. The atmosphere inside

Goodison is intense, especially in a derby game. I was lucky enough to experience a few as a young lad at Everton. I've also experienced the Scouse banter first hand, having lived in a house where loyalties were split. I couldn't understand half the banter though, as this foreign language was new to me.

This morning, having had the game postponed last night, we trained on the pitch at Plainmoor. A full practice game, tackles, shots, headers, the lot. The quality was excellent, there really is some great young talent at this football club. Oh to be that young again. Tomorrow we train again in readiness for our Planes, Trains, and Automobiles trip to Barrow on Friday... snow permitting!

THURSDAY, 5 FEBRUARY 2009

It's a boy

Breaking news! Dan my next-door neighbour, fireman and tennis rival, has just knocked on the door and announced the arrival of his and Jen's new baby boy. Dan has not slept for a day or so but said that mum and baby are great. Well done you guys, see you soon.

Thanks again Jodie, you performed an intricate operation with skill and patience today. Yes, I popped into Jodes Salon in Torquay today and Jodie, a good friend and my club sponsor, took at least an inch off my hair. That is a short back and sides for me. See you in a couple of months.

I visited The South West MS centre yesterday to talk about a charity event taking place there on March 25th. The MS centre, otherwise known as The Multiple Sclerosis Therapy Centre, is a place where sufferers of the disease are given support, help and therapy. The range of therapies includes high-dosage oxygen therapy, physiotherapy and massage to name but a few. The reason I have come across this sort of treatment is that many football clubs and physios now use it for injuries, Specifically oxygen therapy. This

involves breathing pure oxygen through a face mask whilst sitting in the chamber under pressure. I first had this treatment at Brentford. Having torn my calf I had several sessions in the week and managed to play in the fouth round of the FA Cup on the Saturday. Martin Allen, the then Brentford manager, was also very persuasive. Wayne Bridge, the then Chelsea player, was also having the treatment for a broken leg at the time. As well as pampered footballers and their injuries, there are obviously many other cases of people with injuries, such as burns and breaks, as well as MS sufferers who really benefit from the treatment. I have spoken to quite a few men and women who wax lyrical about the benefits they get from the oxygen therapy, especially MS sufferers, who ironically have to be referred to it by a doctor as no scientific studies have been definitive on the results. I remember being in the chamber one time, it was full and one-by-one people were discussing why they were there. 'I have very bad burns' said one. 'I have recently lost a leg' said another, and 'I really suffer with my MS', another added. 'And you?', somebody asked me, and what did I say? 'Oh. I have torn my abductor muscle...it's tough'. The reaction was great, lots of laughter and banter. There really are some brave and humble people out there, with amazing senses of humour. Anyway, Esme, the lady who runs the MS centre, and kindly gives access to the treatment for next to nothing, has asked me if I would be one of their 'prisoners' for the day. Basically I will be 'captured' and held to ransom, I will then phone friends (generous ones) and ask them if they would contribute to my 'release' in the form of money. This then goes to the MS centre, as it is a self-funding charity. So, friends and family please keep your phones on and wallets warmed up, as on the 25th March you may get a call!
The South West MS Centre
01392 447411
E-Mail: info@southwestmscentre.co.uk

Snowed Off/Cook-Off

Obviously with the nation grinding to a halt because of heavy snowfall, it was no surprise to receive the phone call informing us that the game was cancelled. As well as the coach company not being able to get out of Devon, Barrow Football Club declared their pitch unplayable. It has been frustrating in the last week or so, not playing and not picking up points. So, on hearing the news about the postponed trip, it was off to school with the kids in the snow. Snowball fights all the way. Jason and Sarah, friends of ours, also were both unable to work and so popped round to pick up their daughter, Ruby. Fiona looks after Ruby a couple of days a week. Anyway while we were chatting away about the weather, as all Brits do, it was suggested that we get together tomorrow night for a bite to eat. Stupidly I opened my mouth and the words that came out were at best rash... 'I'll cook'. Myself and Jason had mentioned that we might try to attempt a meal each and feeling confident, and now with time on my hands, I boldly said that I would create a three-course meal. Babysitters sorted, I was now firmly committed. Oh God. All I can say is 'what have I done? I must have chosen one of the most labour-intensive three-course meals ever. I could do with Gordon, Nigella, Jamie and Delia helping me, such is the intricacy of the cooking. Oh, and Floyd could come over with the wine! Sorry but gotta go as Harriet is shouting for some more milk (three pints and counting today!) and also for her mum, who is out at Body Pump/attack/step, otherwise known as two hours of peace and quiet. Add to that the fact that I am knee deep in cream and butter (prep, yeah!) it is time to go. Results around 10pm tomorrow.

Hot in the Kitchen

As mentioned on Friday, I had a moment of madness and committed myself to creating a three-course meal for friends on Saturday night - basically the first three-course meal I have ever done. After looking through the 15 or so celebrity cookbooks my wife has, I started preparing on the Friday night, whipping, mixing and chopping a variety of different ingredients. My menu was as follows:

STARTER
Thai Chicken Noodle Soup (Delia)
Frozen Grapes (Jamie)

MAIN COURSE
Lamb Braised in Beaujolais (Delia)
Roasted Vegetables & Dauphinois Potatoes (Gordon)
Appeltiser Lollies (CH)

DESSERT
Banofee Pie (wife)

WINE: Red, white and champers

So we got home on Saturday afternoon at about 2.30pm and I basically stayed in the kitchen getting one heck of a 'dab' on till about 8pm. The lamb needed five hours in the oven and it needed watching like a newborn baby. I asked my wife about a thousand questions throughout the day, all relating to timings and flavourings, not forgetting 'do you know where the Ibuprofen are as my back is crumbling.' To cut a long story short I managed to pull it off and produce the meal. My wife and our friends Jason and Sarah gave it a big thumbs-up but Jason was very suspicious as to whether I had cooked it, especially when tasting the Banofee Pie, which he loved. Well, yes, I created it. But I have to say that the preparation, the whisking, basting, roasting, boiling, freezing, simmering, reducing, grating, crumbling, and in fact anything ending in 'ing' was a big test for me. I think I lost a few pounds in the kitchen yesterday (monetary as well) and by the end of the meal the kitchen resembled the garage - stuff everywhere! Towards the end of the 'cook-a-thon' I felt like I was in charge of 50 spinning plates, each one teetering on the edge before being rescued. All in all it was a pleasant surprise (to me!). Good company... and good food! Would I do it again? Not for at least six months! Anyway, I have done my bit, Jason it's over to you! By the way mate, I know that you have been up to something, preparing a ridiculous feast. Are we going to be digging up some sort of bizarre meat from your garden that has been cooking underground for a week? Are we going deep-sea night fishing, then eating the catch, or do we have to come to yours wearing togas and prepare ourselves to sacrifice a defenceless pig? Bell me if it's a bush tucker trial as I think I may be playing that night!

MONDAY, 9 FEBRUARY 2009

Weather Man!

Will it ever stop snowing, raining and sleeting in Devon? I would rather play in a swamp tomorrow night than have to postpone another game, so hopefully the rain stops and we go ahead. You do need luck in this game, but honestly - is Burton the only place in England that has not been affected by the weather? It wouldn't surprise me if they were expecting a heatwave at the weekend. Anyway, we just have to concentrate on ourselves and make sure we are ready for the last two months of the season. However we do it doesn't really matter, promotion is our only thought. It's not a war cry but every ounce of blood, sweat and tears, from the training ground to the gym to the pitch must go into achieving it.

I will try to switch off from football now and give you the return of 'Statto'. We spend 18 months of an average lifespan on the phone and six months on the toilet. A quick calculation tells me that if you cut your phone calls down by two thirds, then kill two birds with one stone by making all calls whilst on the loo it means that you will free up a whole year of your life. Happy days. Must go as I have a few calls to make!

Loss

All the talk, all the effort and we go and lose at home *(2-0 at home to Weymouth)*. Missed chances, bad refereeing decisions and the inability to keep a clean sheet all added up to a poor night. We gave it a good go in the second half but it wasn't to be. We win, draw and lose together though, and as captain I will look at myself first and foremost. The support was great and although I'm sure it was hard to watch us lose tonight, thanks for the reaction at the end of the game.

Pain in Spain

Spain...2 England...0. The result was fair I think, but in saying that Spain's goals came through bad mistakes and England did have chances. You could tell though that Spain played with the confidence of a team that has just won a major championship. The passing and possession was brilliant at times. I think the introduction of Beckham helped England a little bit, through his passing and vision but also his stature. Other players seemed to raise their game with him on the pitch. On the whole though it did look like one team was really comfortable on the ball and the other not so. Taking into account the fact that the average weekly wage of an England player is about £70,000 you would think that our players would be better than theirs. But they are not. Other European nations seem to have progressed so well in recent years that they sometimes make us look inferior. Our 'up and at em' spirit is not always enough. In the football academies all over England the emphasis is now on being comfortable on the ball anywhere on the field. It may take several years but it will be worth it in the end. Wow, that was a bit serious, eh?

Away from football and I must mention my dad, Martin, whose birthday was last week. Belated blog greetings. Martin Hargreaves Motorcycles ceased trading for 48 hours as my folks went to York for a quick break which, as dad put it, was 'reasonable, son'. I think by 2020 you will be able to start winding down and pottering, dad, but until then there are around 100 MOT books to get through, 300 tyre changes, 50 engine re-builds and around 10,000 cups of tea! Happy birthday to a great man and a top dad.

Funny Old Game

Sam Allardyce gets the sack, Kevin Keegan resigns or gets the boot, Joe Kinnear comes in from the cold and then has to have heart bypass surgery, and now Colin Calderwood, the man recently sacked by Nottingham Forest, finds himself at the helm along with Chris Hughton. Who said it was a funny old game? It certainly is for Newcastle fans. Hopefully for Colin he can turn it around. I worked with him at Northampton and he is very passionate about the game and a decent fella. Talking about it being a funny old game, did anyone happen to watch 'Piers Morgan On' last night? If so, you may be familiar with the format. Piers Morgan, the controversial ex-editor of the Daily Mirror, turned TV host and critic, has been visiting some of the most glamorous, most money-driven places on earth. We are talking Monte Carlo, Dubai and Hollywood. While out there he has interviewed countless millionaires, ex-pats, TV stars and singers about their experiences and views on money and stardom. Last night's offering was in Hollywood and after visiting Sharon Osbourne (pad!) and Mel B, among others, he then asked Vinny Jones how life was treating him. If you don't know who Vinny is, a quick summary - former hod carrier, turned footballer, turned actor. In fact, turned actor who now commands £1million a film and lives next door to Hollywood's A-Listers. After being asked the question 'how's it going?' Vinnie answered "I was riding down Mulholland drive yesterday on my Harley thinking 'where did it all go wrong'" Now that is 'a funny old game'.

As far as we are concerned at the club, it is back to business tomorrow. I can't predict results and I don't want to talk about ifs and buts. All I want to do is go to work and give it 110 per cent, as do the rest of the lads.

SATURDAY, 14 FEBRUARY 2009

Back To Winning Ways

A good win *(3-1 at home to Altrincham)* and a good performance puts us back on track in the league. We slipped up in the week and admittedly we should be winning those type of games. But after two days of decent training and a few strong words before today's game we were back to our best today. Again to the hardcore fans who turn up every week thanks a lot for cheering us on.

On the home front now and with The Beast safely tucked up in bed and Cam and Issy soon to follow (after watching 'Ant and Dec') my wife and I will be mostly demolishing an Indian takeaway and quaffing a few glasses of plonk whilst reminiscing about the old times. MTV on in the background and a few glasses of bubbly now constitutes a top night in. Happy Valentine's to all... the night, as they say, is young!

Up North

On receiving the news that I had a few days off, due to a forthcoming suspension, the car was filled with petrol and children, and was soon thundering up the motorway, heading north - destination Cleethorpes. For those of you who don't know where Cleethorpes is, it is next to Grimsby. For those of you who don't know where Grimsby is, it's near Hull. For those of you who don't know where Hull is, I suggest that you either do a GCSE in Geography, or for ease check out a map of Britain. Anyway, the wardrobes were emptied, the milk was cancelled and we were off. With the football season as it is, and the school term times non-negotiable, getting back to see the folks is very difficult - so any opportunity to do so is welcomed with opened arms. The fact that it is a five-hour drive also makes nipping home an epic event, especially with three children. With the DVD players on the blink and the pack-up being demolished in the first half-hour (by The Beast) the journey was always going to be a test. In fact the relief was immense when we finally rolled in to town after five hours, two service stops, four arguments, 17 shouts of 'are we there yet?' and the same of 'how long left?' Last night we stayed with Fiona's parents, Joan and Iain. Today we headed to my folks, Martin and Avy, to surprise them with impromptu visit. Already the trip has involved, in no particular order, a cooked ham, a fish and chip supper, a trip to the beach, presents for the children, a brunch, two bike pick-ups with Martin (for Cam), a sleep-over and six bottles of wine.

Full report on the 'East Coast Riviera' maybe tomorrow but for now all I can say is that although the weather has been rough in Devon lately, it's cold up north!

Pundit

Apologies about missing a few blogs recently. Yesterday turned in to a bit of a mammoth trip, a 2pm departure from Fiona's parents' house and a 2am return. The trip in question was to Kidderminster for the guest slot on Setanta's broadcast of Kidderminster versus Cambridge. It was a good chance to see two of our promotion-chasing rivals close up, teams we may end up playing again this season. Cambridge won quite comfortably in the end, and I would certainly expect them to make the play-offs. With ourselves having beaten and drawn against Cambridge this season it bodes well for any future meeting. I know Setanta has been criticised in the past, and although I agree some of the fixture structuring hasn't helped us over the last 18 months, you can't argue that it has not given clubs, managers and players at this level great exposure. It is just very frustrating that on the whole we have not played as well as we can in front of the cameras. What I can tell you is that the people who matter at Setanta really want Torquay to do well. We have a big game at the weekend against Kettering, unfortunately for me I am suspended. After 40 games it is very difficult as a midfielder to avoid a suspension - even more difficult when referees give shocking decisions! In their defence though, the Respect campaign has helped, the meeting of players, management and officials before each game does create a calmer atmosphere. In fact at half-time, as I was standing in the tunnel at last night's match waiting to do a bit of punditry, the door of the ref's room opened and I was offered a nice cup of tea! Now that would not have happened 12 months ago. Back on the road today, it's goodbyes to parents and parent-in-laws and off to Northampton. There I will drop the family off for a long overdue visit to friends of ours, I will then head back home to Devon.

Modern Man

Firstly, hi Cam and Issy - we hope that you are having a great time with Luke and Ellie. Secondly, hi Carl and Ange - we hope that your stress levels are holding up OK! Love you guys.

Before leaving for training this morning I sat down and watched five minutes of breakfast TV. And what did I see, you may ask? I saw two ladies explain how they had set up a website, for women, to air their grievances against the male of the species - from snoring to watching footy, from not tidying up to drinking beer, all the classic moans were there. Thus giving them the title for their website 'Moan About Men'. Come on, give us a break, the modern man has almost morphed into his partner. Gone are the days of being able to watch the footy on TV - I am currently watching a set of gnashers being replaced on a 'You Are What You Eat, Be Naked and Happy, Ken Hom's, Gok Wan's Pyjama Party' type of programme, whilst two lots of Uefa Cup games are on the other side. And why? It's easier that way!

It's not enough that we rush round the house panicking in case the there is a rogue crumb on the carpet or that the wardrobe is tidy for an oncoming kit inspection. No, now there is a website for every woman out there to have a go at the 'old man'. Imagine if a couple of lads had set up a website to complain about women? There would have been a public outcry. I could give the two ladies in question a couple of great case studies though. My lovely mum, Averil, was looking forward to her birthday treat. My dad came home and said 'OK, put your glad rags on love, I'm taking you out to buy you a treat'. On arriving at their destination, a local department store, my dad led my mum through to the electrical goods department and said 'go on, pick whichever one you want'. And what was on offer? Deep fat fryers! Classic! Another family classic involved my wife's mum, Joan. Her birthday was approaching and she dropped several hints that a black velvet jacket would be well received as a present. The hints were obviously not strong enough, the present was... an electric carving knife! I have learnt that no means yes, yes means no, and that under no circumstances do you listen when your wife or girlfriend says of an oncoming birthday or anniversary 'I really don't want anything, honestly'. What that actually means is 'if you don't buy me anything I will pretty much not talk to you for three days'. Must go now as my wife wants to check out a website on the computer and I want to get the Argos catalogue out to look up deluxe steam irons.

P.S. Manse - Bevs asked if you were still 'showing the line' at Newton Abbot? Sorry mate, but I am still probably as mad as you. I should have gone across the keeper again for the hat-trick! See you in the morning, Lamby.

FRIDAY, 20 FEBRUARY 2009

Suspension

I am really gutted not to be playing tomorrow. It's a very strange feeling on a Friday night not having a game the next day. It is an even stranger feeling on a Saturday afternoon, not playing. For most players of my age this fear of not playing is the reason we continue to play and want to achieve success in the game. As far as tomorrow is concerned, I am really looking forward to watching the boys as they hopefully hammer Kettering. I will be in the changing room with the lads tomorrow and kicking every ball with them - from the sideline.

SUNDAY, 22 FEBRUARY 2009

Road Trip

The Hargreaves clan have just rolled back into Devon after a 1,500 mile road trip taking in Cleethorpes, Grimsby, North Cotes, Kidderminster,

Northampton and Kettering along the way. Looking back at the game yesterday *(lost 2-1 at Kettering)* it feels like an opportunity lost to gain three points. The game unfortunately was lost in the first 15 minutes though, a bad goal conceded and an unfair goal conceded meant for a tough afternoon. Although Kev scored a great free-kick before half time and the fact that we were by far the better team in the second half, the damage had been done. As a team we have to start getting clean sheets again, hopefully starting on Tuesday. This week, for the family, has been full of reunions, good food and good company. Staying with old friends towards the end of the week has been great. Carl, a mate from my Northampton days, and his wife Ange have treated us like kings this week. They have recently moved to the village that we lived in near Northampton for four years, before our pilgrimage to Devon, so staying there brought back good memories and a few reunions. When anyone comes to visit us down in Devon I always have the itinerary ready - beach, walk, park, forest, abseiling etc. I have finally realised that after a five-hour drive maybe visitors just want to relax. So when Ange was nervously looking at me each morning ready for a random shout of 'are we ready then, because the canoeing school shuts in three hours' it must have been a relief for her to see me sat down. I find it very difficult to sit still but I have to accept that a 10-mile hike through a forest in the rain is not everyone's cup of tea. So instead of the usual gruelling outward bound mission, we sat down and chilled out while Carl made his famous pasta dishes - famous for the length of time they take to reach the table, the record being a smidgen over five hours! Harsh mate, great job again! The hospitality is second to none and the fact that I am offered a job in parcels every time we meet (usually by Ange about 11pm and with the help of a little 'Wodka') reassures me that I will be able to get employment if I ever stop playing. As well as the Andrews' hospitality there is also the 'Get out of jail card' service that Carl provides. This can be used during the early hours for car breakdowns (me and a burning Renault Laguna), it can be used for house moves (Fiona wanted no breakages), and it can be used for extreme rescue situations. The most recent being for Ange who, after a few social sherries, found herself stranded in the middle of town. She phoned Carl to come and get her, when he asked her where she was (this is brilliant) Ange held up her mobile phone and waved it about, saying 'I'm here'. Obviously at this stage Ange's phone did not have a tracking device in it, but guess what? Unbelievably, within no time at all, Carl 'Columbo' Andrews was on the scene. He had found Ange and was soon returning to base. Now that is service for you. Thanks for this week you guys, see you in Devon soon, hopefully along with our other long lost friends - Rob & Kate, Helen & Ian and Nina & Tony.

Finally, I spoke to Broughy yesterday and he was delighted with the last two games at Salisbury. Two wins and two clean sheets, after a 4-0 defeat and a conceded penalty (by Broughy), is a great boost for him and Toddy, who is also on loan there. He told me that Toddy is still on form. In a recent phone conversation Toddy was agreeing with a friend that a player he knew was a bit up and down form wise - Toddy said 'yeah, he really does blow hot and cold, in fact he's like a hot potato'. You can't buy that banter, you really can't.

TUESDAY, 24 FEBRUARY 2009

Pre-Match

Not enough hours in the day yesterday to post, so apologies about that. Tonight we face Forest Green in a game that we need to win. I will resume this blog post-match, hopefully with three points in the bag.

Score Draw

What a night. We started the game really brightly, taking the lead with a great strike by Matt Green, but within the space of a few crazy minutes we found ourselves 3-1 down at home (to Forest Green). Two poor goals conceded and a ridiculous penalty meant that we were up against it. Scoring just before half-time gave us a bit of hope but the half-time team talk was still a bit fiery. What is said in the changing room between us stays between us and is said for the right reasons. It has to be forgotten when the whistle blows again, and it was. Credit to the lads as the second half performance was spot on. To be honest, the first half wasn't that bad, we just got punished for slight errors. I have to say that even when we went 3-1 down the fans stayed with us and cheered us on, so a big thanks for that. I don't want to be returning home after drawing 3-3 with Forest Green and neither do the rest of the lads or the fans, but that's how it is. It will be back to the training ground tomorrow to sort it out. I overheard a footballer the other day moaning about his treatment at a club and of his life being tough at home at the moment as he is out of the team. Well cheer up mate, you have a couple of hundred grand in the bank and there are - believe it or not - a few people worse off than you. I was walking the kids into school the other day and a young mum of four lively children mentioned that she had seen me on TV the same day as her husband. I asked her why her husband was on the box. She explained that he had been filmed along with his fellow soldiers on tour in Afghanistan. He has seven months on and two weeks off. So the children will see their dad for two weeks in April and then he will be off again for another seven months dodging bullets, car bombs and grenades. I reckon he would settle for being a footballer out of a team at the moment.

Spit and Sawdust

Extremely tired tonight, so a lightning-quick blog. With last night's game over it was back home to watch late-night TV, eat, mull over the match and generally get no sleep whatsoever! As usual, the caffeine intake meant for a rough night. I crawled in to bed around 3am after watching several episodes of 'Shameless' but within minutes Harriet had appeared and had begun the ritual of wriggling around the bed whilst occasionally ramming her foot or arm into my head. I decided to nip next door to Issy's room but fared little better there as she seemed to be break dancing in her sleep. I actually considered going for an early morning walk but I dug in and got two hours sleep before the school rush started. It was good therapy going in to the club today though, not for a massage or a stretch, no - the therapy came in the form of throwing weights about for an hour and a half. Sometimes turning the music up full belt and hammering a few weights out is the perfect remedy for a tired and angry man. I have spent a lot of time in gyms over the years, from spit and sawdust hardcore dungeons to Lycra-filled social meeting clubs, but they have always given me the same pleasure, anger release time and thinking time. I know this is not always the case for some, so apologies if the post-Christmas, pre-summer, morning-after-the-night-before workouts are not having the desired effect. Sometimes a cup of tea and a packet of Dunkers is the only way forward. Covering all bases, the kettle is on and I am heading for the biscuit barrel.

THURSDAY, 26 FEBRUARY 2009

Food and Drink

It may be unusual but, as I am typing away, I am watching the final of Masterchef. The three finalists are competing to win the crown of top chef, and with it a pretty-much guaranteed job in the industry. It's amazing how this programme sets the old hunger pangs off. I have chosen a full-on pasta dish, Cam has gone for tomato soup and Issy a hot chocolate (bizarre choice). Poor old Harriet would have been in her element. The same applies to shopping for food. If you're hungry while shopping it's game over as your trolley will be ram-packed with all sorts of delights. It is 'Barron Greenback' in the Hargreaves household at the moment, though. As far as the cupboards are concerned they are definitely bare. Yes it's diet time! Fiona, my wife, has eradicated all forms of carbs, sugar, and wheat from the kitchen. I am surprised the kitchen sink has been left. The only thing remaining in there is air. I have had to nip out to Tesco on a need-to-survive basis tonight. To be honest though, for anyone who goes on a diet the last thing you need to be seeing is someone tucking into an industrial-sized family bar of Dairy Milk or a vat of pasta. In saying that, surprisingly enough Fiona has gone out with a friend tonight for a meal. I can just imagine her ordering... 'I'll have the royal burger please, but could you lose the fries and the mayo, in fact lose the burger and the bun and I'll crack on with the rest!' I have told her a million times not to diet but as soon as she has put down another copy of 'Heat' magazine, it's time to for me start stashing emergency supplies. Can you imagine the run-up to Toddy's wedding?

FRIDAY, 27 FEBRUARY 2009

Marathon Man

A strange kick-off time, an old club, live on TV and I cannot wait. Yes, we are in front of the cameras again in what is a tough game. Oxford have been on a great run of form but these are the games, as a player, you want to play in week-in, week-out. You have to try to enjoy your football, otherwise it can drive you mad - so no predictions, ifs and buts, crystal balls, tea leaves, or signs in your water. We are going there after a solid week's training and what will be will be. That is as long as we win, of course.

I popped in to Jodes salon for another short back and sides today - an inch off all round. I am though, slowly but surely, preparing myself for the 'big' cut. I am seriously considering getting the fleece sheared for the summer, the only thing that is stopping me at the moment is the fact that I want to run the London Marathon. The reason I need my hair long for the 26-mile slog is all in my proposed outfit for that particular day. Running the marathon dressed as Tarzan definitely requires long hair, so maybe I'll run it but tie in a haircut at the end of the race. There is also the small matter of the football season still to play out. All these influencing factors are conspiring against me, sorry Jodie but for now it's still a pair of scissors and not a set of clippers.

At the club today we had a little bit of an 'old school' morning, doughnuts and tea before training accompanied by the odd story from the lads (Damien was on fire!) Also knocking about was a programme with a picture of me in from 1990, which went down well for comedy value. Anyone with a Beatles haircut and shorts as high as a pair of Speedos would sympathise with me. It did get to me a bit though when one of the boys said that he was two years of age when that picture was taken, and some were even younger! I told the lads the first 15 years are the hardest, the rest is a breeze! Once they start getting near me in pre-season I'll start worrying (willpower and the 'elbows out' technique gets me through). Anyway, on the doughnut count we had most of the lads on one, Kev on a half, Mark Ellis on three and Tyrone last seen smuggling his fourth around the back of the changing room. Danny Stevens used his as an inflatable ring, one of the balls went into the dyke and so he jumped in to get it. The Bevanator just smelled his doughnut, Damo just licked his and I think Elliot may have opted for the doughnut facial. Good times.

TV Win

The summary of last night's game? Great performance, great result, great night *(beat Oxford 2-0)*. We needed to win and we needed to win in front of the Setanta cameras. I'm sure that result and performance will give the players and supporters alike a lift, as in recent TV games we have definitely not done ourselves justice. Oxford have won their last seven games at home so to go there and end that run and to do it on 'the box' feels good. Thanks again to our supporters who travelled to the game and cheered us on, it is much needed and much appreciated. I met up with lots of old friends from my time at Oxford last night which was nice. There are some really good people associated with the club and hopefully before long their league status will be guaranteed. For now though Torquay's league status is first in line.

Today's diary of events will involve the purchasing of school shoes, the demolishing of a roast pork dinner, the voting of where to go on the Hargreaves outward bound mission and the general healing of a very sore body.

Mood Swing

Tonight I am officially in a bad mood. A bad mood for me still means that I can make the children and my wife laugh and that I can function, but what it also means is that something/someone has annoyed me. It won't last long, as I can't afford to spit my dummy out at home or at work, but it will have an effect on tonight's blog. That effect will be evident in the amount of words I type. With the 'game on tomorrow night, different atmosphere but same importance' shout done, the amount of words typed is about 90, and with a good night and a God bless it will just about top a ton.

Journeymen!

Not a few hours training, not a nine to five... no, yesterday we put in a 16-hour shift. The Stagecoach left Devon around 11am and returned around 3am. Welcome to the real world, eh? That the coach resembled the 'Night of The Living Dead' towards the end of the journey or that some of the lads got off the coach still in the seated position didn't matter. We won (2-1 at Grays Athletic) and at a very difficult place and in torrid conditions. The wind was howling and the rain lashing down (no, I'm not telling a ghost story). Before the game the referee had explained that both sets of players were to stand for a minute's silence for a devoted Grays fan who had recently passed away. I have never seen a tighter group of players during a minute's silence.

At one point I think Bevs and Wroey were actually hugging me for warmth. With Grays fighting for their survival in the league, with the wind swirling about the ground and with a six-hour coach journey behind us, all usual excuses were there. Not last night though, we were committed to winning and returning to Devon with three points in the bag and that is what happened. An amazing turnout by quite a few hardcore Torquay fans. Standing (or jumping up and down) in the wind and rain must have been testing. A victory was the least we could do. In summary, a very long day. But in return the lads got three points, ate a combined total of about 90 bags of sweets, got through around 10 different films, sent around 1,000 text messages and abused Dave, our driver, 215 times (destination Grays, stopping at Leighton Buzzard, Shepton Mallet, Melton Mowbray, Hartlepool and Dundee).

P.S. Second posting around 8.30pm

Second posting

Apologies if this posting contains some mistakes, as whilst typing away, I am watching, and a bit sidetracked by, Heston Blumenthal's Victorian Feast. He has already constructed a drink based on the one that Alice drank in Alice in Wonderland. The drink that made her shrink. It contained toffee, hot buttered toast, custard, cherry tart and turkey. The general consensus was that in the hedonistic days of Victorian life, five out of six families used opium and that the book itself was based on one long drug-taking experience.

So, back to yesterday. The coach ended up looking like a crime scene with bodies strewn everywhere. Damian and Kenny were asleep at the front on a lilo, Tyrone was wedged in between bags and seats, Robbo was cradling Danny, and even my film partner Stevie 'Ghoul' Adams had abandoned me halfway through the final film to join his friends in the world of the unknown. Mark Ellis actually fell asleep whilst playing Football Manager. I was too busy replying to Scotty Bevan's texts (three seats away) to go to sleep. The big man is still hating the fact that, during the Setanta interviews last Saturday night, I gave the viewers the 'Pec Dance'. He reckons I stole his thunder, even though his desperate attempts at walking past the camera five times didn't work. I've told him that I will get him on the blog again, and in fact manage him if he decides to go for UFC, WWE or boxing glory. What more does he want?

Today I took Hatty on the train. We chatted away about life and food. I think we were both having two different conversations but it was great. Her vocabulary is definitely varied. Shouts of 'that's ridiculous', 'for goodness sake' and 'really tremendous', combined with 'I'm not a petal, I'm a Hatty Beast' made for a funny afternoon.

THURSDAY, 5 MARCH 2009

Jailhouse Rock

After a pretty intense training session it was a surprise to see so many faces in the weights room. Normally there are only a few of us left in there, but today the gym was teeming with lads pumping iron. Now I could say that with our season hotting up and with games coming thick and fast, the boys are getting in a bit of strength training for the remaining few months. Or I could say that summer is just around the corner and that the old abs, pecs and biceps need a bit of shaping for the beach. I think the jury is definitely out on this one.

News flash: Funnily enough I have just overheard a news flash on '60-Second News'. Ashley Cole, the Chelsea and England footballer, has been arrested outside a bar in the early hours this morning. He was allegedly using threatening behaviour and swearing at police outside a London nightspot. Meanwhile his wife is in Africa climbing Mount Kilimanjaro and raising money for Comic Relief. Now I'm no saint but come on mate, is being a millionaire, playing for Chelsea and England and having a pop star wife not enough? Why don't you park up the Bentley, buy a few £300 bottles of wine or, what the hell, even Crystal, and have a night in with the boys.

Get the cards and cigars out, set the pool table up, turn the jacuzzi on and take the cover off the pool. Last of all turn the old jukebox on and kick back and relax. Just don't play any Girls Aloud tunes.

Rally

I arrived at Newton Abbot racecourse today to find lots of motor enthusiasts gathering, for what at first looked like a bit of a car club. It turned out to be some sort of South West Rally, starting with a lap around the racecourse. This was just too much of an opportunity to miss, as, parked in the corner of the car park was our physio Damien Davey's car. It was early and while Damien was busy treating the sick, and most of the Halfords-loving car enthusiasts were busy checking out each other's Peugeot 106's, Rover 14's and Mini Metros, the time was right. With my right-hand man (Kenny Veysey) in tow, we set to work on Damien's car - the perfect car for a rally, 15 years old, one not very careful owner, no working instruments and the length of a barge. Yes, the Mercedes 'Boat Class' was kitted out with personalised number (69) and large DAVEY letters on the side. It was then driven to the start enclosure and abandoned. It was like a core workout for me and Kenny watching people admiring the motors on show and then getting to Damo's barge and looking round it a bit confused. We were in stitches. Most of the lads then arrived and we all had a good laugh as Damo (when told of his car re-positioning) donned his overalls (complete with sponsors logos) and cap and proudly stood by his car while I presented him with the 'Best newcomer but most likely to break down' award. It's just a shame Damien had to work, and we had to train, as seeing him being counted down 5...4...3...2...1 go, go, go would have been priceless.

Tomorrow we face Rushden and Diamonds in the league. An old mate of mine, Andy Burgess, from my Oxford days will be in their line-up. I will try my best not to kick him but obviously accidents sometimes happen. A fellow card school member at Oxford and Soccer School partner in Northampton, Burge is a really nice lad. We had some great laughs at Oxford, even in the dark days, and although he has been through a lot in the last couple of years his philosophy in life still remains the same: 'Deal with it in the morning'.

P.S. Happy birthday tomorrow to Martin 'yes, you did train well today' Rice. Twenty -three tomorrow, so the least I could do today was buy Ricey a coffee and a sandwich. You can square me up next week pal.

Bad day at the office

Not happy tonight, not happy at all. Not only should we have won *(drew 1-1 at home to Rushden)* but the results around us went our way, and so it has to be said it is three points dropped. I'm not sure how people in other jobs react to a bad day at the office but I know how it affects me. Weekend ruined.

Another mammoth trip for us on Tuesday, this time to Altrincham. Already the only thought on my mind is winning there and until we play the game my bad mood will remain. Other than that I hope everyone out there has a great Saturday night and weekend.

Adrenaline Junkie

I have just read an article on base jumpers, madmen and women who just love jumping off mountains and, more often than not, skyscrapers. Recently a Frenchman and an Englishman climbed the 155 floors of Dubai's newly constructed, and the world's biggest, 'Burj' skyscraper. At around 5.30am, after a short look over the building site that is Dubai, they leapt off the half-mile high building. They landed, escaped security guards and lived to tell the tale. It may just be me, but whenever I am at the top of a big building or bridge the first thought that pops into my head is that of 'wonder what it would be like to jump off?'. No, I have not got suicidal tendencies. It is the same instinct that jumps into your head when, at a wedding, or a school assembly or even a dinner party, you think about shouting 'blah blah blah blah' at the top of your voice! Maybe that one is just me. There must be a line though that you, or your mind, crosses to do something that is beyond the risky. I'm talking jumping the Grand Canyon on a bike (Evil Knievel), or climbing into a barrel and being pushed over Niagara Falls. Or in fact, as in Phillipe Petit's case, to walk across a tightrope between the Twin Towers. Incredibly, Phillipe Petit evaded security to rig up the thin piece of wire, attaching it to both towers, before walking across the 30-yard gap. He didn't do it once, he walked it 11 times in 40 minutes with only a 25ft balancing pole for company. My wife and I actually went for a meal at a restaurant at the top of one of those towers and it was a long, long way down. I think the reason people do these crazy stunts is sometimes for fame but more often than not for the rush of adrenaline you get. That is why I have pencilled in the skydive, the white water rapids, climbing Everest, wing walking and the purchasing of a Ducati 996 (maybe that one is a mid-life crisis). For now though, the combination of Red Bull and the pre-match bell is enough adrenaline for me.

WEDNESDAY, 11 MARCH 2009

Last Gasp

A late return back to Devon in the early hours of this morning but a return to Devon with three vital points *(won 1-0)*. Again a mammoth coach journey, this time to Altrincham, a team fighting for their league status. A last-gasp goal was no more than the lads deserved, especially Wayne Carlisle who has shown huge character in the last few weeks. A good pro works as hard when he is out of the team as when he is in it and by doing that old Wayno has been rewarded with two winning goals in a week. Travelling fans, we thank you again. I'm sure a few of you were tempted to get away early but the combination of a lack of any home fans traffic problems and our away form meant staying till the end was a good option. All we can do from now on in is to win as many games as possible and deal with whatever comes our way with a strong mentality.

Marital Bliss

Evening all. It will be quick and painless tonight as 'Comic Relief Does The Apprentice' is on. Flicking through the paper today I was astounded to see the attendances at the big European games this week. Over 80,000 fans for Roma v Arsenal; Bayern Munich v Sporting Lisbon attracted 66,000 fans; Man Utd v Inter Milan 75,000 fans, and a massive 93,000 fans saw Barcelona beat Lyon. Incredible numbers at these big games and also a real presence again from English clubs. Once again it will be hard to bet against an all-English final. More incredible numbers have been bandied about in today's papers as Bernie Ecclestone (the Formula 1 boss) prepares to give his wife Slavica a £1.2billion divorce payout. On the grounds of 'unreasonable behaviour' by old Bernie boy, the quickie divorce will certainly put a dent in the F1 supremo's pocket. On the upside, he will still have £1.2billion to play with. If Fiona and I ever face the prospect of a divorce I will obviously leave her the house and car, and I'm sure in return she would be more than happy to leave me the bike I'll probably have by then, the dog I'll probably have by then, the contents of the loft and garage, and more importantly and without doubt the delightful array of credit cards.

FRIDAY, 13 MARCH 2009

Looks can be deceptive

Cam, my son, is sat on the sofa watching his favourite TV programme, Top
Gear. Harriet is destroying a bottle of milk next to him. The other girls,
mother and daughter, are having a girly night out with friends at the
cinema. That leaves me to put the children to bed, eventually, and then sit
down to wade through the third series of Prison Break. As with most of
these American dramas, take your eye off the ball and you're suddenly 30
episodes down, so while I can it's a case of sofa, bloodshed and tattoos. I
have given up on Lost - the plot on that programme is not thickening, it's
actually set, and I haven't even seen 24 or the other popular one I can't
think of that everyone watches. The thing is we Brits accept these decent
American imports and just enjoy them, whereas the Yanks take our best
stuff such as The Office and completely nause it up. I'm surprised they
haven't Americanised The Royle Family with old Jim sporting a set of
whitened gnashers and Barbara breast implants. Going back to Prison
Break and tattoos, I took my little firecracker Hatty, or Hatty Beast as she
calls herself, to the supermarket this afternoon. While there I had to remind
her not to stare as she was fixated on a couple of lads in there. But as I
turned round to see what she was so interested in, I found myself doing the
old 'Goggle Box' and 'Neck Brace', such was the spectacle. Now I don't mind
tattoos, in football you come across some real beauties - Chris Todd's Welsh
flag, fist and stars; Manse's nursery rhyme and Chinese takeaway order;
Northy's bulldog, and even an old mate of mine John Ashton's Ten
Commandments, completely covering his back (even though he has never
adhered to one of them in his life!). But what I saw, and what Harriet was
so intrigued by, was in a word, mental. We are talking massive, ear to ear,
spider's web chin strap, creeping ivy growing up his back to the top of his
head, a teardrop below both eyes and, to cap it off, two earrings the size of
fifty pence pieces wedged in between his ear lobes. Oh, and his ears were
covered with ink for good measure. I don't know if he was popping in for a
pint of milk or a pint of blood. In saying that, looks can be deceptive. In my

Northampton days I walked into a Jaguar garage with my long hair, ripped jeans and beanie hat on. I was nearly escorted off the premises. Yet when one of the lads from the workshop recognised me as a Northampton player the kettle went on and the finest dunkers came out. I also remember going back home to Grimsby to help my dad out in his garage and workshop. Complete with overalls on, oil on face and a pick-up for wheels, I stopped at a cashpoint. As I was waiting for the old spondulix to appear, a couple walked past me and I overheard the guy say 'Jesus, that's Chris Hargreaves - he used to play football, and for Town as well. Look at him now, what a loser'. I was actually playing for West Brom at the time!

On to tomorrow and as ever it is a very important game. We will concentrate on ourselves and nothing more, and hopefully by this time tomorrow we will all be one game nearer promotion.

SATURDAY, 14 MARCH 2009

Home Front

A much-needed home victory today *(4-1 at home to Barrow)*. There is a lot going on at the football club at the moment on and off the field, the only thing that remains constant is the need to win. That was done and now, as usual, it is on to the next game. No anecdotes, no stories, just a recharge of batteries and back to work next week.

MONDAY, 16 MARCH 2009

Take-Away

Our fierce 'cook-off' rivalry, with friends Jason and Sarah, was put on hold on Saturday night as we decided to do take-away. The choice of Indian was made and after we had all returned home from victory at the game, a double celebration on the day as Jason and Sarah are huge Liverpool fans and so had two 4-1 victories to cheer, the call was made. We ordered big, and with the liquid refreshments in place we were soon tucking into some seriously spicy dishes... then disaster.

Sarah was immediately struck down with 'Delhi belly', having to lay on our bed within minutes of eating. And no, it was not a bizarre plan to get Tarzan upstairs, she was really poorly. I hadn't had a drink and so dropped them both off, taking it easy round any sharp bends. So, the one time we go for a take-away someone falls ill. To be honest though, Sarah thinks it was a case of a 24-hour man/woman flu bug. Nevertheless from now on it's strictly 'cook-off' and Jase has now got me very, very worried on that score. It was my turn last time and, although I do say so myself, it wasn't half bad. But old 'Topper' Miller has gone one massive step further. He has not only sent an invitation out but there is a theme. On the invitation, to 'The Sultan's Banquet - Morocco' no less, we are asked to dress appropriately. So it's a Moroccan loin cloth for me and my wife, a night of mysterious food and a guest appearance from Sid the snake. Just a normal night really.

TUESDAY, 17 MARCH 2009

Issy

Happy birthday to Isabella Eve Hargreaves, nine years old today. Those nine years have gone very quickly. The birthday celebrations started with the cinema on Friday and ended with a meal out tonight. Times have definitely changed as her presents included getting her ears pierced and getting a netbook. I dread to think what purchases await in another nine years. As long as I still have a job and there are no boys around it will be fine. We love you very much darling and are so proud of you.

P.S. Happy St Guinness day to all.

Steve Woods

Obviously, unless you have been on Mars, if you are a Torquay fan the news that Steve Woods is no longer at the club will be common knowledge. Woodsy is a top lad and a good player and will be missed by all the lads at the club. We have had a good laugh over the past 18 months or so, and as founder members of the 'old school' we have had a common bond.

Although I have been speaking to Steve, I just wanted to wish him, and his lovely family, all the best for the future from myself and all the boys. Cheers mate.

Taxi for Hargreaves

Hargreaves Taxi service has just returned from the football, athletics, back to football, back to athletics, back home run. Not that I'm a pushy parent or anything but when Hatty (now aged two) takes up tennis it is going to get really busy. This week's training has been unusual in that the sun has made an appearance. Mark Ellis actually got burnt during this morning's session. It wasn't that hot but Mark's body is only designed for cold weather. Between Stevie 'Ghoul' Adams and Mark there is only a three-minute window of sun allowed before the old factor 100 has to come out. As I mentioned a few weeks ago on the blog, the gym is packed at the moment, especially this week, as the boys can smell the beach. The Bevanator's weights sessions are increasing weekly, in fact the barren spell that he is enduring with the female of the species is getting that bad that he has resorted to some bizarre gym one-on-ones. He is regularly asking Wendy, one of our masseurs, to pepper him with punches for a minute. Bevs tenses up while Wendy punches away on his stomach, gloves on of course, for a minute. That, coupled with the fact that he is constantly asking Mark Ellis to wrestle with him, sends massive alarm bells ringing.

We leave for Northwich tomorrow and aim to return late on Saturday night with three points in the bag.

Battle

Relieved to be back home in good time tonight. A real battling performance from the lads saw us rewarded with another crucial victory *(3-2 at Northwich Victoria)*. My room-mate Chris Todd returned, and what a return for him it was, a great performance and a goal to cap it off. As well as his presence on the pitch, the banter in our room last night was epic. I'm delighted for Toddy and I'm sure his family are extremely proud of him, now he just needs a promotion medal. Further goals, a brilliant header from Sillsy and a winning strike from Rosco, on his return, sealed the victory. The game got a bit heated at times, on and off the pitch, but that sometimes happens, especially when one team is fighting for its league status and the other is fighting for promotion. Today's game certainly was not pretty but the points are all that matter at this stage. A great following and a great win all the same.

MONDAY, 23 MARCH 2009

Mothers Day

Belated blog 'Happy Mother's Day' to Averil Hargreaves, my lovely mum, and to Fiona Hargreaves, Cam, Issy and Hatty's lovely mum. After the lie-in, breakfast in bed and presents, the decision was made by the Hargreaves clan to have a day out in Woolacoombe. Sun, sand, and surf was enjoyed by all, as was more breakfast, some waffles, a bit of shopping (expensive day, this Mother's Day business) and the building of a few hundred sandcastles.

Father and son did manage to get a few kick-ups in on the sand but it's hard to sneak off with three strong-willed women in the family.

We trained today in preparation for tomorrow's game against Grays, again a team fighting for their lives. We know it will be another tough game, but it is also another game that we can win. On to the fitness front now and the 'Bevanator' is close to breakdown after this weekend's events. A chocolate sponge at the hotel on Friday and a McDonalds on the Saturday, coupled with a few comments in the gym today that he has lost his shape, have really thrown the big fella. I think he could still be in there now working on those crunches, he looked that worried. Don't let them (I mean me) get to you mate. I must admit though, Friday's evening meal was a killer. I ordered Bruschetta to start and out came cheese on toast. I then ordered the pork and out came a full fry up with chips, and for dessert, it was too late by then, the chocolate sponge was on its way. Another player who has been throwing the old weights about is a real surprise. Not a hulking defender, a battling midfielder or even a big centre forward. No the D-Unit, Danny Stevens, has caught the bug. A combination of a desire to play every week and an imminent Ibiza 'large one' has seen Danny hit the iron hard. Dennis Wise watch out. Lastly Mark Ellis has finally got a bit of colour to his skin, unfortunately though it is not down to the sun. The showers on Friday were only a couple of degrees below boiling point which meant that it was a quick in, 'ow', and back out several times. But with Mark loving showers as he does, third degree burns didn't worry him at all. As long as he spent the nine minutes 48 seconds he requires daily in there, the fact that his skin was melting off was not a problem. While I'm on the subject of 'Dingle' I have to say that his attitude this season has been spot-on. It is not easy for him, or any player, to be in and out of the team but when he has played he has been ready and when he hasn't he has been the first one to shake the lads' hands and wish them good luck, not an easy thing to do. The competition for places is strong, and although not everyone can play each week hopefully come the end of the season we can all celebrate together, as that is what this squad has been - very much together.

Thanks to all

A very long, bizarre, but productive day. It started with Harriet jumping on me at 6am ready to get up. This after a bad night at the office and not much sleep. I don't need to say much about the game (drew 1-1 at home to Grays Athletic) as it was said for us by the fans at half-time and at full-time. We were as disappointed as anyone and although we have had a great run, a draw at home at this stage is frustrating. We didn't play well, end of story, and will look at why tomorrow.

The rest of the day was a blur. I was picked up at 9.45am in a fire engine and handcuffed for a 'ransom' day at the South West MS centre. I then spent four hours on my mobile phone asking lots of friends if they could donate money to ensure my release. I managed to raise £1,200 pounds for the MS centre and for all those poor unsuspecting people who received calls, a massive thank you. In all, along with several other 'hostages', we managed to raise £5,500 pounds for a great cause. I then nipped in to Jodes Salon with Kev Nicholson for a trial run of a traditional wet shave and man's facial treatment. Jodie, my sponsor at Torquay, asked us if we would pop in to try out the men's treatments available at the salon and then put a bit about it in the salon's newsletter. Jodie and her husband John are huge Torquay fans so maybe it was a bit of a risk, after last night, letting Jodie loose with a cut-throat razor. But I have to say, even though it was a first for both of us, Nicholson and Hargreaves left unscathed and feeling great. It was then back home for a bit of tea, then out the door again for coaching and back in about 9.30pm. A tough day, especially after last night's events, but for everyone who will benefit from that five-and-a-half grand it was well worth it.

Anyone for Tennis?

I have to first apologise for the lack of blog postings in the last few days. Thursday night was spent filling out tax returns (nice), last night I was at the hotel, had forgotten the old laptop and wasn't prepared to spend £24 for internet access. That leaves today... I'm back, so here we go. A hard-fought draw today against a tough new-look Mansfield side and even tougher weather conditions. It was more like a game of tennis in the middle of the park today, the ball was literally going from head to head for the whole of the first half. A good second-half display and a great debut goal from Blair Sturrock at least gave us some reward for the lads' efforts. Blair is on the lookout for a good hair restorer and owes me money for cards, but other than that he is a really good lad who is going to give us some more firepower for the run in to the end of the season. Thanks from the lads and staff for the support we had today, in very cold and windy conditions we were cheered on until the end. I have returned home to find my wife in bed (yes, on her own) and with the house still showing some signs of the party the night before. A friend of ours, Sarah, had her 'pre-hen night hen night' last night and it was hosted by Fiona, who I've heard partied like it was 1999. Believe it or not, the bride-to-be made sure everyone got home and in to bed! Fiona made it up to bed about 2.30am and Hatty Beast arose at 6am, that has got to hurt. Still, I'm not complaining - the house is quiet, I have just finished off some great leftover party food and cake, and I can stay up and watch as much bad late night TV as I like.

P.S. Bevs - stop sending me pictures of your abs and concentrate on the job in hand. And definitely stop doing press-ups before you take the picture. Trying to end the one of longest barren spells ever known should be your only thought...

Sleeping Lamb

A late picnic on Exmouth beach, an even later fish and chip supper at Budleigh Salterton, and now a small/large glass of red will finish off a nice Sunday.

P.S. They say football is a funny old game, well Formula 1 is giving it a good run for its money. Almost without a team, written off as a serious racer, and constantly in the shadows of fellow Brit Lewis Hamilton, today's winner was Jenson Button. He must be feeling pretty good in his trailer tonight with Richard Branson in tow after winning his first race for Brawn. He is also still earning a fortune, even after agreeing to take a £4million-a-year pay cut.

P.P.S. On the way home from Budleigh, Harriet, our two- year-old firecracker, looked out of the window and said 'look at all those sheepies'. She carried on 'where's Manse? Is Manse in there? I can't see him, is he asleep?' (a reference to our very own Lee Mansell). Sorry Lamby, but now even Hatty has caught the bug - every time she passes a field she thinks you're in it!

Random

The Clarke's Nutcracker can remember 700 of the 1,000 seeds it buries over 100 square miles. The seeds it can't remember will grow into pine trees. Sorry, was I speaking out loud there? Just watching 'Yellowstone' which is on in the background and what a crazy place it is. America's 'wildlife jewel in the crown' has some of the hottest and coldest temperatures in the world, from boiling hot geezers to -50 degree winters. I know, I know, I have to stop it for fear of boring the whole of Devon. Last night I watched Secret Millionaire. What a great programme it is, last night's episode saw a scrap yard owner-cum-millionaire visit Blackpool. He was a big bloke who knew his way around a fry up and at first glance you would probably never have guessed he was very rich, but he was. After infiltrating a homeless centre, a 'Dream' house where terminally ill children and their families could have a holiday together, and finally a war veterans club, Gary was brought to tears at least five or six times. He had lost twin sisters to heroin abuse and had been brought up by his granddad, who was a D-Day landings hero, so he had experienced first-hand the pain these people he met had felt. It was a great sight, when at the end, Gary announced that he was a millionaire and that he wanted to give the respective parties thousands of pounds, great TV.

Then we watched Piers Morgan on Ulrika Jonsson, just slightly different, but interesting all the same, especially for John Leslie, Stan Collymore and Sven-Goran Eriksson.

Today, a day off and an epic skill school with the boy. Father and son outside with Torquay 'Hargreaves 14' shirts on enjoying football like we were kids again. Well, one of us anyway! Finally I feel like I need to tell it like it is. I have played every game but one this season, and yes I am shattered. So to the bloke who shouted 'come on Hargreaves, get a *******
move on' at last week's game, I say fair enough. If I had had a hard day at work and had put my money in my pocket to watch Torquay only draw at home then I would be annoyed. And yes I would probably be shouting at the captain. So when my three children are in bed and I have trained all week and played my 44th game this season at the age of 36, I will definitely have tried to get a move on. If the pain of last season still burns you and not a day goes past that you don't think about it, then fair enough. No one is more desperate than me for promotion this season, and whether I am at Torquay or not next season I will be doing everything in my powers to achieve it, end of story.

TUESDAY, 31 MARCH 2009

NFL Super Skills

I have spent the last 30 minutes trying to post a video on the blog. It is not working so I am now giving up, before I beat up the laptop in anger. Just go into YouTube and type in NFL SUPER SKILLS. See what you think!

WEDNESDAY, 1 APRIL 2009

Arts and Crafts

Two heavyweights in the football world met today. Baby Sills and toddler Hargreaves spent the morning together. While Hatty helped her Mum 'look after' the bambino, we took to the training field for a session. With competition for places fierce, the standard of training was good - crossing and shooting, followed by a fiery five-a-side. It is the way training should be, competitive but not reckless. Those who step over the mark will only get away with it once. It is incredible how quickly this season has gone, three weeks or so and the season is done, well almost.

Another big weekend is nearly upon us. Yes, Saturday night we are heading to our friends for a Moroccan banquet, complete with belly dancers, velvet cushions and hookah pipes. Oh, and we also have two massive games in the space of three days to look forward to.

Tomorrow sees the start of the Easter break for the children. This break is marked at school with an Easter Bonnet parade. As always, all the parents will be up all night sticking and gluing, no doubt desperate to achieve the 'Best Bonnet' award. We will be no exception, having relentlessly paper mache'd our way through the week. Has that paint dried yet?

28/03/09

No blog as such tonight. Just a dedication to Lee Hodges and his family. Lee was informed on the journey back from Mansfield that his dad had died on Saturday after the game. A very difficult remaining hour or so on the coach for Hodgy, as we still had not reached home. Hodgy is a really nice lad, who still, even at this difficult time, came in yesterday with a smile on his face as he always does. To Lee and family from all the boys, our thoughts are with you.

Banned

I cannot actually believe what I have just seen on the news. Scotland captain Barry Ferguson and Goalkeeper Alan McGregor have been banned for life by the Scottish FA for inexcusable behaviour. First came the news that they had gone out the night before this week's World Cup qualifier, the manager discovering on waking that they were still in the hotel bar. They were subsequently dropped. But this is not the worst of it. Incredibly, whilst on the bench for the Iceland game, both players were visibly giving the 'V' sign and the bird to the cameras. It was like watching Kevin and Perry Go Large. Unbelievable, a gargantuan lack of respect shown by these players. The Scottish fans were in uproar, as was the FA, and now both players have been banned for life for playing for Scotland, Ferguson just five games short of getting into the hall of fame. His Rangers manager, Walter Smith, looked lost for words. All the best in the SPL games next week lads, I think we may see both players in the Premiership soon.

Other news in bullet point form tonight, and in no particular order. Obama asks for back-up from European nations in Afghanistan, Shearer returns to rescue Newcastle, Hamilton disqualified from the Australian Grand Prix,

Todd wins 'Face of Slaters' award in Swansea, my mate JD is playing for Kettering tomorrow and looks like Paul Nichols, and finally Mark Ellis and Scott Bevan wrestled today and as usual Bevs won.

Aperitif

A good win *(Kettering at home, 2-0)*, a Moroccan banquet and a day at the beach with my family. This, in a nutshell, was the weekend. I will elaborate in around half an hour. Back to the game and a great day all round it was. We played well, other results went our way and there was a great following to cheer us on. Another big game tomorrow, regardless of what happens the belief in the squad of getting promotion, through any route, is very real.

An awesome display last night, this time from our friends, Jason and Sarah, who have taken the cook-off to a new level. Not only did we enjoy an unbelievable lamb and date tagine but the house was decorated in true Moroccan style, complete with low table, cushions, hookah pipe and throws, all accompanied by music straight from the set of Turkish Delight. Jase (Topper Harris) must have sweated his way through most of Saturday to create the feast but it was well worth it. We have now decided though that it is time to calm down on the cooking front, to keep topping each other is tough. I was actually thinking hog roast for the next do, complete with medieval costume, fire eaters and silver goblets of wine. This will have to wait as the next cook-off is suspended in favour of an easier option, a table for four please! The only downside to the night, as far as Jase was concerned, was that I topped him with the old outfit. Sorry about that pal, I had to do it. My parents, Avy and Mart, have been down all weekend and we have absolutely loved it. They have spoilt the children rotten, as usual, and were also at the game which was great. It all went too quickly though, so roll on the summer.

Outside Chance

Another fantastic night in front of the Setanta cameras, what an atmosphere created by our supporters. Winning last night against Burton *(1-0)* has at least given us an outside chance of automatic promotion. If that does not happen then we are on a great run of form going into the play-offs. The run-in will be full of twists and turns, tonight being no exception, with some of our promotion rivals playing against each other. Gotta nip out now but later on I will give you a lowdown on yet another horrific coach journey, more about the game and other random information.

Later on

We arrived at Burton Albion's ground after one hell of a battering on board the yellow peril. Not only did we have to contend with seats made out of concrete and covered in scouring pads, but yesterday was special, even for the yellow submarine. With two drivers in tow we felt that it would be a pain-free trip, but how wrong can you be? The toilet was out of bounds, with the remains of last weeks rotary club trip to Bognor Regis swilling about in there it was like the loo area at Glastonbury. That smell, combined with Elliot's continued stomach problems, is still with me now. But surely we would be quick with two crack drivers... No, we left Pete Morgan at Michaelwood services by accident - he was queuing for a creme egg at the time. This was only discovered after 10 minutes so Pete was panicking - he jumped in with a couple who had seen us leave, firing up the motorway at top speed. In the end, after a great chase and an hour round-trip we picked him back up at the same services - he passed us twice in the car! Pete was also crocked for the game after hurdling the central reservation! So now we were really rushing to get to our pre-match meal. After seeing both Burton and The Belfry signs go by, alarms bells started to ring. Maybe they knew a different route. But after a discussion between Hargreaves, Sills and Nicholson it was decided that I would give them a gentle nudge at the front. I pointed out that we had passed both destinations to the drivers. After a

152

quick shuffle of a map (no satnav on the banana) and a reddening of cheeks we soon were pulling off. They had gone 30 minutes past the junction, to be fair an easy mistake to make, especially considering there were massive signs saying Belfry and there were two of them looking. Another hour later we ate a late pre-match, had a few Rennies, and then soon after arrived at the ground broken. It worked again though, a great away performance by the lads. Five hours on a mobile toilet can't even break us.

P.S. Nice to have Becky, Andy, Josh and Millie down to see us. With nine people in the house it's going to be fun.

THURSDAY, 9 APRIL 2009

Wind Machine

Unfortunately I ran out of time to post a blog yesterday. The Hargreaves and Carrington clans had an appointment at the beach, then later on I had an appointment with the clunk and click master (chiropractor), and, to finish off, the brothers-in-law watched the second half of the football in 'The Slaughtered Lamb' - you know the one, open the door, everything stops and the locals stare at you as if you have two heads and a tail. Our two families set off for Woolacombe. It was great for the children to see their cousins, Josh and Millie. The lads' car arrived at 12, the women's at around 10'clock. Fiona thought she knew a short cut, but unfortunately the road was blocked and then they got stuck behind a hearse for 40 minutes. Eventually all the children piled in to the sea and had an hour on the bodyboards, then, as is the way, we destroyed the sand sandwiches. The migration to the shops (not for some!) followed this, then the time was right. I had persuaded Andy to get a board and suit, and, while no one was looking, we sneaked off to hit the waves. Andy had never surfed and I hadn't been for 10 months so the signs were ominous. We spent the next hour drinking sea water. It was like a washing machine in there, the wind machine was on and the waves were harder to read than tea leaves. But we still loved it. Then it was back to the ranch for 20 minutes before shooting off to see the 'back quack' for me, and finally, for us both to see the football. I know everyone wants to talk about Burton, promotion and/or the play-offs etc, but we are just trying to concentrate on winning the next game. In between games if you can try to turn off from everything it does help, but that is easier said than done. Great to see the young children from the supporters' trust at training today, I'm sure they all enjoyed firing shots past Ricey. It was good for us to finally see some of Danny's classmates. The only trauma for the children was seeing Bevs shoulder press one of the little fellas.

FRIDAY, 10 APRIL 2009

Tom Dick

Only a few words tonight, I'm not feeling great so it's early(ish) to bed for me. Simply two huge games to win and 17 Easter eggs to get through this Easter break.

SATURDAY, 11 APRIL 2009

Overdrive

The run is over, but, after having won eight and drawn three of the last 11 games, to lose to Crawley at home (2-0) is a big blow. Maybe it has ended our chances of the title, but obviously until it is mathematically impossible we live in hope. With other teams winning around us it is now vital that we cement the play-off place. To be honest, I'm on overdrive typing this. I'm absolutely gutted that we haven't won because winning every remaining game was the aim. The lads have been giving it everything, and even in today's game although we were not quite at it we should have had at least a draw, with us having six or seven great chances. The problem is that we have had no room for error, constantly playing catch-up after our bad start. Like everyone I'm a bit low, the trick is though not to be too gutted. We have to be ready for the play-offs, ready to win them and then win at Wembley.

Watching

Not much chat on the return journey tonight *(drew 2-2 at Salisbury)*, just a lot of ifs and buts. Again we had a chance, but the title now cannot be ours. We are back on the training ground tomorrow to sort out yesterday's and last Saturday's problems, and also to start to prepare for the next game. Watching from the stands today was very difficult, as was hearing the other results coming in. A day in the life of a fan was not an enjoyable one. But what is done is done now, play-offs it has to be, the thought of lifting a trophy must drive us on. I don't intend to rip my hamstrings apart, play over 50 games or put my family through hell for nothing. I was left with a difficult decision today, play and risk tearing my hamstring, which would mean end of season, or not play and hope we win. Damien, our physio, pretty much said that it would be madness to play, but sat here now, feeling like c*** is not much better. Another win will seal our play-off place, then we will worry about the play-offs.

Epic

What a game. With my boy Cam supporting Chelsea and my mate Jase supporting Liverpool, it was a tense night. I used my expertise before the game, saying 'it will be tight here, Chelsea will be solid'. Spot on, eh? Eight goals on the night and 7-5 on aggregate in the end. I had to put earmuffs on

Cam in the end as Jase was getting hot under the collar. To be fair though, this is a man who was in Istanbul on that famous night to see Liverpool's epic comeback, so he was expecting big things again. It wasn't to be though and Cam was delighted, now they just have to beat Barcelona. I managed to get him to the last Chelsea v Barcelona game. Was it because I had a connection, or was it perk of the job? No, a friend of mine worked for Barclaycard and he got some free tickets. A professional footballer could not get a ticket from the FA. As Roy Keane said, 'the prawn sandwich brigade were still in their boxes wining and dining when the second half kicked off'.

Family always comes first...

I have received some very sad news today so no blog tonight.

Witching hour

It's 3.30am, I can't sleep. I've got three layers on, plus a blanket and I'm shivering and sweating. No I haven't been out on the pop, I am in the grip of some sort of flu. Last night, or two nights ago now, we stayed in Stevenage. The Welsh dragon (Chris Todd) slept continuously, up until around kick-off, while I beat up my pillow up and slid off my wonky bed. Eventually I got up about 7am, leaving Toddy fast off - this is the man who, after being told he had leukaemia, slept like a baby for 10 hours leaving his family up all night. The flu had set in, my body was in shock. I forced some breakfast down, had about five vitamins (nothing compared to Bevs' daily cocktail of 17 bad boys), went for a walk, had an ice bath (bizarre choice), and then returned to bed until we had to leave for the game. Great prep for a big game, but it didn't matter, we were all up for the fight, as were the fans who I have to say were brilliant, non-stop all the way through. It really lifted the team, especially in the second half when we were down to 10 men. We still had chances but it wasn't to be, a hard-earned point it was *(drew 0-0 at Stevenage)*. Another five-hour trip home, Match of the Day and a cheese sandwich completed the day (tough at the top, eh?). Now a trip to Barrow awaits, victory there should ensure our play-off place. The top of the table is tight but we have the games in hand so it's up to us. I don't really know if any of this is in order but I will sort it out in the morning, which by The Beast's clock is about three hours away. I'm now going to consume my own body weight in flu tablets.

P.S. Happy belated birthday to lovely my mum, Averil. Love you lots and see you soon. Tell dad not to come to the Burton game on the bike if it's raining.

TUESDAY, 21 APRIL 2009

Road Trip

Huge game tonight for both teams for very different reasons. We will be travelling back through the night tonight, so three points will make for a smoother and more comfortable journey. We will of course do everything in our power to win tonight so full match and journey report tomorrow.

WEDNESDAY, 22 APRIL 2009

Final game decider

Shock horror, it's a final game decider. An eight-hour journey, followed straight after by a training session on a car park pitch, was just what the doctor ordered. The game itself was tight, a point for two days of hell seems harsh *(drew 1-1 at Barrow)*. A few words were said in the changing room after the game, I really hope they hit home for Sunday. If you are sat on the beach in the summer and you can say to yourself I gave it everything, on and off the pitch all season, then fair enough - I hope for everyone that that is the case. The return journey was like a scene from a horror movie with bodies everywhere. Rolling back into Devon doubled up at 5.15am was nice. The only thing that kept me going on the trip back was our card school, good honest lads who will all be digging in again on Sunday. Thanks to all the fans who travelled to the game. If I could pay for all your travel expenses I would, because that was a trek, but Mrs Hargreaves' budget doesn't have enough in it. I'm sure the Burton players and staff were gutted to see our result come in, to be honest it's the last thing both clubs wanted (a final game decider). We will obviously go to win the game and for the Setanta cameras it could not be better. With my family coming down, my boy wanting to go to Wembley and myself in need of a job at the end of the season it should be a real stress-free weekend.

OK now onto another tense subject, the Player of the Year award. Last year I was honoured to receive both awards, voted for by the most important people - the fans and the players. To captain the side for the wins against York, which enabled us to play at Wembley, was great and to play 50 games was also a real plus. Missing out on promotion hurt, probably too much, but that's life. My thoughts on this year's winner will remain private but I really hope that the recipient gets it for the right reasons.

THURSDAY, 23 APRIL 2009

RV

A bit of light entertainment tonight - me and the missus are watching Katie and Peter - The Next Chapter. They have moved into a Malibu mansion, Pete has just bought a Porsche and the children have just received the entire contents of a toy shop. Is it shallow? Is it tacky? Who cares. Come on, if you or I had the money we would be there like a shot.

I took Harriet and Cam to see some motorhomes today, Fiona and I had been an hour earlier as well. It was great, these things are awesome – two-berth, four-berth, or like the one we spent the most time in, an eight-berth beast. Cam and Harriet were jumping in and out of the bunks and I was checking out the toys on board (Kev, you will be pleased to know that they have full shower facilities). We were looking for three reasons:
1. The in-laws are looking into buying one.

2. Our friends Jason and Sarah are borrowing an all-singing, all-dancing, plasmas-on-board RV for a road trip next month. With me being co-pilot (Meet The Fockers) I need to be ready.

...and 3. Well, no reason really.

One thing is for sure, cheap they are not - but what a great laugh it would be rolling up in one, complete with surfboards, bikes, the lot. One of the best holidays I had as a child was in a 'home-made motor home'- our family and another in a Ford special. It was a long wheelbase Transit van, complete with two double mattresses in the back for the children, a swivel chair in the front, welded in by my dad, and about 20 cases on board. What a holiday, an 18-hour trek to the South of France and we loved every minute of it. I spent the next two weeks snorkelling ridiculous distances (nearly giving my parents a heart attack) and eating French bread and jam - bliss. It's either the sea air down here, or my age, but I have even thought about getting a beach hut.

P.S. St George's Day, 23rd April. A drink will be raised today for St George, our patron saint. Hopefully with a bit of a resurgence this will again become a day of celebration and rest - as it is we celebrate Ireland's patron saint more than we do our own! Tomorrow we train and it will be geared around one thing, beating Burton.

Up and down

Some teams have survived today and some teams have been promoted, others' fates still hang in the balance. This is the time of season where all that hard work during a season can be rewarded with success. We hope that tomorrow is our day, and that the following three games see us promoted. Tonight though it's a case of relaxation (easier said than done). With my parents coming down for the game, and my children there tomorrow as well, a victory against Burton is my only thought.

SUNDAY, 26 APRIL 2009

Play-off place

What a day. One team gets beat and gains promotion, the other team wins and seals a play-off place *(beat Burton 2-1)*. Well done to all the lads and staff, their efforts can now be rewarded with something this season. For me to score was special. A goal in the week at Barrow with lots of emotion swirling inside was important for me, and then today, to have my family and friends at that end of the ground when I notched was amazing. I can honestly say though that I have never been in as much pain on a football pitch as I was today. A torn muscle in my back in the first half meant that the last 70 minutes of that game hurt like never before. I actually remember tracking back for a cross in the second half and blacking out. It's madness, this game. Four injections today got me through (I had two before the game for a different injury), thanks to Damo, Pete and Andy for all your help. Well done to Tim Sills as well today, who battled on after a very nasty knock. Great to see you Avy and Mart, love you lots, see you at Histon. Massive rest and recuperation needed now. Thanks to all who cheered us on today, the only focus for us all now is May 17.

Delicate areas

Cam is riffing away on Guitar Hero (I have just had a go and bombed big time), wife and Beast have taken Issy to dance, and on their return I will take the older two to athletics - back to normal in the Hargreaves house. Today at the training ground Pete Morgan and his team of sports therapists at South Devon College were kind enough to visit us, a bit of TLC never hurt anyone.

Yesterday we met up with Kev (Nicholson) and Jenny, who is expecting at any time, to discuss babies, money, football and jobs, oh and food! Jenny is going for a home water birth, so, in true Nicholson fashion, the baby will have no choice but to wash at least five times a day. The birthing pool has been set up already so Kev has been doing a few lengths each morning, complete with armbands and rubber duck. Again, sorry mate I can't help it.

Other than that we will start to prepare for Friday's game against Histon tomorrow. Hopefully the atmosphere will be the same as last Sunday. I have basically been recovering and trying not to walk like Steptoe, whilst taking the odd happy pill and icing continuously. On Sunday night, when the dust had settled and the Hargreaves clan were tucked up in bed, I turned on the TV. Lazily, instead of making the hourly pilgrimage to the freezer, I decided instead to use one of the chemical ice bags (you know, the ones where you squeeze a pouch and the bag turns ice cold), settling in with the ice bag in place on my back. I had forgotten all about the pack until, after about 40 minutes, I started to get one heck of a burning sensation in some really delicate areas. I had been sat on it that long that the bag had burst and its chemical contents had leaked down my back and into areas that, let's say, don't normally burn. I hadn't moved so fast all day (some may say including the game). I shot (fast hobble) into the kitchen and literally sat in the sink. I wouldn't say that there was steam coming off body parts, but what I would say is that I did then go to the freezer and have to ice parts that don't ever normally see ice!

Life

Lots going on at the training ground today, not least a hardcore sparring session and a sighting of the Phantom of The Opera. With Bevs being out of action at the moment with a pulled calf (he is blaming it on me because I shouted at him at Barrow to kick it harder - he did and he tore his calf! Sorry mate) he is now full-on in the gym. Not only is he hammering the weights and sit-ups (much needed), he is also forcing Mark Ellis to wrestle him on a daily basis. To top that, today he put Wendy through hell in a sparring session, she said she tired in the fifth round, that's when he started picking her off with jabs. His behaviour is becoming worrying, judging by his daily lists including things like 11am snacks - peanuts and protein drink. It is high time he found himself a girlfriend. On the injury front, Sillsy returned today complete with a Phantom-type mask, cape and magic underpants, a great sight. I am half expecting him to fly through the air on a set piece tomorrow night. Obviously tomorrow night's game is huge but we are going into it confident that we can get the right result.

Tomorrow will be an emotional day for the family as James will be buried. At 17 years of age and with the world at his feet it is such an enormous waste of a life. He was a fantastic lad who had just taken up an apprenticeship at British Aerospace. You couldn't wish to meet a kinder more fun-loving family and I'm just so, so sorry he lost his life. Although I can't be there in body, all my thoughts and love will be with you Becky, Paul and Hannah x.

FRIDAY, 1 MAY 2009

In Memory of James

James Carroll 1992-2009

Half time

A decent result last night *(beat Histon at home, 2-0)* gives us a good lead
going into Monday night's game. The second leg will still be very tough
though so we must take nothing for granted. Today was a varied bag with
Bevs lifting weights in a Petr Cech-style headguard, Wayne having a
sponsored massage, Kev showing all at the beach (a game of cricket, a quick
dip in the sea and a medicinal pint is definitely good for the soul) and
Manse eating his own body weight in sausages (comfort eating as Michelle
is in Marbella). Tomorrow we set off to Histon aiming to finish the job.

One step closer

It's 2.30am and I have just returned from Histon. Well, almost. I had to nip
back to the services, where we meet, after an SOS call from the Plymouth
crew - Damo had lost his keys so I have given them my car to drive home in.

What a game. I am absolutely shattered, but also absolutely delighted that
we have got through these two games *(lost 1-0 tonight, won 2-1 on
aggregate)*. Friday's game for me was a blur. James' funeral was at 2pm
and my Mum said that it was the saddest thing she has ever witnessed. A
mother seeing her son of 17 buried is just horrendous and I couldn't get that
thought out of my mind all day. I had to do my job though, and that was to
try to help the team to victory. Obviously with the second leg now done, and
the tie won, God willing we are just one win away from the Football League.
I don't think I have ever headed so many balls in one game in my career. It
was relentless - long throw, corner, free-kick, goal kick, and back to long
throw again, for 90 minutes. The boys were magnificent though, as were
you fans who cheered us on all afternoon. Every time we defended another
'bomb' into the box, a huge cheer could be heard. If ever there was a 13th

man it was today. Thank you to everyone who travelled to watch us, you were brilliant. I have to say a huge thanks as well to my family, and, on behalf of all the lads, to their families. Any wife or girlfriend, mum or dad, son or daughter will tell you that footballers never turn off from football and are more up and down than a yo-yo. At least now we are all one step closer to a stress-free summer. It has been a crazy month really, at one point thinking we could go straight up, then being on the edge of the play-offs and now winning the semi-final. The last two seasons have certainly been entertaining. The pain of last season has driven me, and I'm sure many others, on. I hope it is our destiny to win it this year. Until then let us all enjoy this small victory. Sleep time.

WEDNESDAY, 6 MAY 2009

Tactics

I have just been thinking about Monday's game against Histon and I have come to the conclusion that they did everything in their power to beat us. Let's not forget the fact that we also had the 'pleasure' of watching another team come back from a two-goal deficit just hours before we faced a team with a two-goal lead (I'm thinking playing the games at the same time would be just ever so slightly fairer). I'm not just talking about the long throws, corners and free-kicks - that comes with the territory. No, what I'm talking about is the flooded pitch (rumour has it they had a hose on it at one point, not just a sprinkler) which Kenny and Shaun said at one point was nearly unplayable, the gritted pitch which was like falling on to a gravel pit, and the 'stare out' tactic. This was where John Beck, their assistant manager, came into it. For those of you who can't remember him he was the manager of the Cambridge team that threatened to get into the Premiership at one point. I remember playing there for Grimsby in the early '90s and it was the same then, cold showers, no running water and a pitch that could have doubled as a sand pit. As we arrived at the ground and walked towards the changing room, Beck was there, arms crossed, fixed look, staring at every player who walked past. I just smiled and said 'hello mate, how you doing?' but Mr Todd went one better. Yes, Toddy's dad had roamed into the tunnel area looking for refreshments. He saw Beck, who he hadn't recognised, and asked him 'excuse me mate, do you know where I can get a cup of tea?' Brilliant! Old Becky snapped back 'yeah, in there somewhere'. Good work Mr Todd. Whatever they threw at us we took it though, but I have to give credit to their players after the game. Straight after the final whistle their captain, and the player I was up against all afternoon, shook my hand and wished me good look in the final. He was obviously gutted but I think he knew that we had stood up to the bombardment and deserved to get there. It's hard to be humble in defeat but the Histon players were, and whether they agree with their own management's tactics or not, they gave it one hell of go. We now have a couple of days off to recharge the batteries and turn off from football, then we will return to training and prepare for the final.

THURSDAY, 7 MAY 2009

Full day

I'm not sure which is tougher - a nine-hour day, 90 minutes of football or 11 hours of Harriet Hargreaves. I have just clocked off after taking on the last of these options. Obviously I am only joking, I have loved having Hatty Beast today but I can definitely sympathise with all those mothers, and some fathers, who look after their brood on a daily basis. I have been a bit pre-occupied lately, so another one of my nicknames, of 'Superdad', has been neglected. Today, and in the next few days, that is to change. Hatty and I started this morning at Bear Feet play centre in Newton Abbot. We drank, ate and played for an hour or so, but before long we both had itchy feet (no pun intended) and needed a change of scenery. So I drove to Teignmouth, where we took on the play park on the seafront at full pace. After another 45 minutes we were again in need of refreshments so we walked up to the Beachcomber Cafe. I thought it would be a case of a coffee for me and a drink and snack for 'H' but you don't get a nickname like 'The Beast' without some reason. Before long, Hatty was tucking into her preferred choice of sausage and chips (let's not mention my all-day breakfast - I sent a picture of it to Bevs and he sent one back of himself, top off, doing weights). We then headed back to base to plan the afternoon session. I decided that the morning's activities had been a bit steep at £20 (especially considering that Fiona was on the loose with the credit card) and so attempted to entertain all three children for free. We picked up Cam and Issy from school and travelled to Budleigh Salterton. Once there we started with a flask of hot chocolate and doughnuts (51p for three at Tesco) all cuddled up with a blanket watching the waves crash in. Then the clan chased the waves in and out for about an hour. After that we committed to a hike up the coastal path. We eventually returned home about five - job done. Fiona then returned, we all had some food and then they all took off to the gym, athletics and footy run. Lastly I rigged up a mountain of furniture for 'H' to jump off and onto the bed (it used to be a step ladder for the other two but Fiona banned it), gave her a bath, read her a few stories and put her to bed. It may have been a long day but I love those crazy kids. Saying that, I am pleased to be back into training tomorrow.

Cruel game

John Terry must be hurting this morning after seeing his Chelsea team lose out to a great last-minute strike and an incompetent referee last night. I took my son Cam (a Chelsea fan) to watch the footy and for 92 minutes we sat there comfortable in the knowledge that we would be watching the final with Chelsea in it. Well almost comfortable, because after 20 years in this crazy game I know how matches can turn, and to be fair, in his short football life so far, my boy does too. As soon as Essien swiped at the ball my instincts set in and I shouted 'trouble here'. Two seconds later and the ball was nestling in the Chelsea net, with it ripping the hearts out of the Chelsea players and every non prawn sandwich-eating true Chelsea supporter. After seeing his team be one penalty kick away from the European Cup last year, his and his dad's team be nine minutes from a play-off final and then lose a cup final, Cam was surprisingly, but understandably, philosophical about the night's events. He just smiled and said 'that's unbelievable, but what do you expect from a Norwegian ref? What good ever came out of Norway? Fishing and sledging'. Very harsh I know, because for anyone who has been to Norway they will know that it is a fantastic place with great people, but from a 10-year-old's perspective that was his take on the ref's performance. I'm sure much worse will be said over the next few days though.

FRIDAY, 8 MAY 2009

Weekend off

We trained on the pitch today, a good high-tempo session with the lads all buzzing and ready for action. A few press-ups later and the morning was done. Tonight is going to consist of a homemade curry and a bit of Johnny Ross. It is a strange feeling on a Friday night with no game the following day. I have said before that playing football is a bit like being inside or being in the Army, with the regimented training every day, the discipline, and the institutionalised feeling (big word I know!) that you have. It is scary to imagine life without that routine of training and of playing games. I'm not saying that when I stop playing (in years to come) I will head for the nearest prison or Army barracks but I'm sure it will be difficult to adjust. This is probably why so many players go into either coaching or management, or on the flip side struggle to cope with finishing and turn to drink. Having no trade to fall back on is a common problem for many. In the short term though, having a Saturday off does have its benefits. Tomorrow will involve a stress-free morning, lots of coffee and cake and then a few hundred falls off a surfboard. I have toned down my extra-curricular activities to surfing as back in my motocross days I pushed it too far on a few occasions and actually ended up missing a few games - no club mentioned and the season was effectively over, but nonetheless trying to explain a battered ankle after a weekend off was tricky.

Girls' day out

A non-football day today, I don't even know who won and lost in the
Premiership this afternoon (I'll watch it when Fiona goes to bed in approx
45 minutes). No, today consisted of entertaining the girls. Cam stayed over
at a mate's so I took the girls to the ice rink and then swimming - surfing
will have to wait until tomorrow. I watched (too risky to join in) while Issy
flew around the rink and Fiona dragged Harriet around, both on the verge
of hitting the deck at all times. We then all jumped in and splashed around
in a freezing cold pool before heading home. Thanks Bunny for looking
after the boy and Jason for picking him up, by the way the fish and chips
were awesome. That's it tonight, other than to say to all have a great
Saturday night.

P.S. Huge congrats to Stevie and Natalie Adams, who have just had their
second child named Jack. Lovely lad, great family.

P.P.S. Random, but I have just watched a top programme: 'Claire Richards
- My Big Fat Wedding'. Claire (of 'Steps' fame) tries and succeeds in losing
six-and-a-half stone for her forthcoming wedding. A really down-to-earth
girl who tells it how it is and is genuinely lovely, as is her bloke who is a top
fella. This is the sort of stuff I am subjected to regularly but on this occasion
I have to say I actually enjoyed it.

Tiger

We trained on the pitch today which was good, a decent surface makes a big
difference to the session. I'm not saying the racecourse is that bad but let's

just say that Tiger Woods would have a heart attack trying to read the greens there. Great to see people at the ground today buying tickets. I know they are expensive but if it makes you feel any better, most of the players will be a few quid down after Wembley. What with the hotel and tickets last year, I reckon I was around £300 down. And did I enjoy the experience? No, you gotta win it! I will blog again later as the Hargreaves residence is currently a total madhouse - too many kids and not enough staff.

TUESDAY, 12 MAY 2009

Warpath

Belated congrats to Kev Nicholson and his future (although she may still change her mind) wife Jenny. Baby Jessica-May was born on Sunday morning at 6.34am. Kev was more traumatised than anyone as he had gone 24 hours without a shower, but Jenny was a star, not only giving birth but also supporting Kev in his time of need. It is a really exciting time for them, they are going to make a top mum and dad.

Now a few clues - a Toblerone, a bottle of red, a bottle of aftershave, and a homemade cake, eight cards, some money, four phone calls and five texts. Any ideas? No problem, 37 years of age and 20 of them as a professional footballer, yes it is my birthday. A lovely day was had, some nice pressies, a hat-trick, two skill schools (one with Danny S and Pokey for Setanta and one with my boy), and a family tea complete with homemade chocolate cake (The Beast blew all the candles out in one go). I also popped into Jodes Salon, Jody gave me a short back and sides (one inch off all over) as usual. I love it in there, obviously I am not a massive fan of haircuts, or in fact being touched, but, if you want to chill out, have a coffee, and indulge yourself for a while (i.e. Mrs H) then that is the place to do it. I will have to sign off early again as we have a slight emergency. Harriet has learnt a naughty word and is shouting it all around the house. The older two are laughing and making her say it again and mum is losing it. Dad is on the warpath.

Philosophy

Apologies about the lack of blog posting yesterday. I thought I would have time last night but it was quite a late return home after attending the question and answer evening, put on by the Supporters Trust, at the club. The player of the year awards were given out and then it was time to face the music in the form of a Q&A. Only joking, it was a great night, lots of interesting stuff from the select panel - some good questions and some even longer answers (apologies again about my mention of Mansell's dodgy DVD's, they are not X-rated). The one thing that stood out for me, apart from Hilly's answers and Frank O'Farrell's stories, was the goodwill for Sunday's final. I was also asked about the blog and my philosophy on life. My answer on that subject is short - don't ask the Lord for anything, just thank him if you receive it! A strange thing happened yesterday, could it be a sign? I was walking into Starbucks with my wife and The Beast. A lady was exiting the premises and so I held the door for her - she actually held it for me at first but you know, ladies first etc. Had I have shot in first, the outcome would have been very different, my wife or the lady in question would have received the bomb. The bomb I am talking about was in the form of **** and from a great height. A mutant seagull that I think had been on the pop for the last week, and eaten at every fast food takeaway, covered me in you know what. I am talking about my whole (mock) leather jacket entirely covered. I was lucky it didn't land on my head. I had to fold the jacket up and then drop it in the sink to clean it when I got into the shop. No, that wasn't enough. Harriet then decided to throw her Babyccino over me. I know it is a good sign to be **** on, and in my career I have been many times, but it has definitely put me off Starbucks. It was already in my file under megalomaniacs (those who want to rule the world) along with McDonalds and Tesco. Don't get me wrong, I love a frothy coffee and the odd Big Mac, and we do some serious hours in that big store. But, in order, the £9.50 it costs for two coffees in Starbucks and the shouts I hear in there of 'I'll have a skinny, frothy, de-caf, no cream, latte with a shot of vanilla to go please' really wind me up. As does the question 'any pastries with that, or perhaps a cake?' No, let me breathe! Then there's the home of the biggest weasel of all, 'Ronald Mac'. I will smile when I want to thanks, and no, it's too late to throw the old salad chestnut in now, the damage is done! Finally Tesco. Again don't get me wrong, we frequent that place a lot and it is cheap, but it's the wartime-type panic that sets in when one house gets flooded, the 0.001 pence you get back after every tenner spent and the constant stream of people determined to spend their lives reversing in the car park that gets me. Bring back the corner shop, the bakers, butchers and candle stick makers. OK, I'm done now!

P.S. Jessica-May Nicholson is awesome, well done Jenny. Oh, and you Kev!

P.P.S. Massive belated HAPPY BIRTHDAY to Tyrone Thompson for last week. 'The Bunionater' has yet to bring the cakes in, but I for one will not hold it against him - as long as he brings them in tomorrow. Ty is a top lad and a top pro. He has been a real example to all this season, no moaning or sulking, he just does his job with a smile on his face and he does it well.

FRIDAY, 15 MAY 2009

Packed

Tomorrow we set off to Wembley. The match boots are packed and the training is nearly complete. The lads have looked sharp and ready this week for the task ahead - to beat Cambridge and bring the cup, and with it league status, back to Torquay. It will be a tough game but if we play as we have done recently then we will have a great chance of winning. I desperately want to win this game, for my family, the fans, and everyone concerned with the club, as do all of the players. I hope more than anything that the next time I type away on this blog it is to talk about leading the team to victory. Until then...

P.S. To all my family and friends - chill out, no stress, see you after the game.

Promoted 17/05/09

I have waited a long time to write this blog and I almost cannot find the right words to express how happy I am. Happy for every person who supports Torquay and happy for my family and friends who have been there through so many ups and downs. We did it! Those three words are the words that I have waited to say. I have said before that there hasn't been a day that has gone by that I haven't thought about last year's play-off loss, but it is so true. Seeing all those faces in the crowd yesterday cheering and then seeing my family and friends in tears at the final whistle was incredible. It was always going to be a tense day but the lead up to the game had been pretty low-key so the nerves were kept to a minimum. To lead the team out, score and then lift the trophy as captain was the ultimate for me. I will never forget the moment the ball nestled in that net - neither will a few of my mates, who had quite a few quid on me to score the first goal at 25-1! We have all heard the saying 'it's the stuff of dreams' but it was for me. I am so proud of the lads, who were absolutely magnificent. It was a big day for them but they rose to the occasion and fought to the end. It has been a long, hard slog since the heartache of last year, so for the players, staff, and fans of this club yesterday was truly well deserved. My heart goes out to the Cambridge fans who have suffered at Wembley twice in succession and to their players, who will be devastated. But there has to be a winner and yesterday it had to be us. I couldn't have returned home to Devon without that cup for so many different reasons, the biggest being that of seeing my children's faces had we lost. I could talk about it all night long, I am so, so delighted, but after having only two hours sleep - what a great coach journey home, that cup got used to great effect! - I will sign off. Thank you to everybody who has supported the team and to all the people at the club who work so hard for us, especially Kerry – you're a real diamond x.

P.S. I cannot stop smiling!!

Time to relax

I woke up today and for only the second time (the first was yesterday) in about six years I could relax. I bet you're laughing now reading this, mum, because I know you and dad will be feeling the same. Winning the game at the weekend has meant that this summer can actually be enjoyed, and why? Well, I'll run you through the last five or six seasons (in equation form) to try to explain.

Last season's last two games: play-off loss + cup final loss = summer of discontent.

Season before, last game: play-off loss + on penalties = end of Oxford.

Season before, last game: relegation to the BSP (Leyton Orient sent us down and were promoted, I had declined their very good offer to join them at the start of the season) = depression.

Season before, last game: play-off loss + chance of a return to the Championship = major groin repair + a sad farewell to Mad Dog (Martin Allen understood that the five-hour daily commute was killing me) and lots of pain.

Season before, last game: play-off loss on penalties + shocking ref (we had overturned a 2-0 deficit to be leading 3-2 but in the last minute of normal time the referee got confused and gave a free-kick the other way resulting in a goal) = tears and my last game and last goal for Northampton Town after four great years.

This season, last game: play-off final...WIN + no penalties = total and utter joy!

As you can see, the ups and downs in football can be huge, so to be able to pick the paper up and see the team on the steps of Wembley picking up the trophy is bliss, plus my wife can now go on holiday! Before I forget if I could list all the people who have helped me this season it would take a long, long time. Thanks so much to you all (you know who you are), as well as the 11,000 fans who came up from Devon to the final and the countless others who willed us on at home. Finally, someone said to me after the final that they had seen a huge change in me in the final games of the season. No real stress, no pre-match Red Bull, no wearing studs (boots!), and even no pre-match meals. My attitude had changed dramatically from one of doubt and uncertainty to one of hope and belief. It's not melodramatic and it's not a crusade but I couldn't get the loss of James out of my thoughts. He was so young, with so much ahead of him and here was I worrying about my football. I hope you were up there looking down on that game mate, because I have certainly looked up a few times in the last few weeks.

Epilogue

And so here we are, 20 years after my debut against, of all teams, Cambridge and we have beaten the same team to win at Wembley and gain league status.

I have thoroughly enjoyed writing these blogs. It has been like a kind of therapy for me - not the sort of 'Mr Hargreaves, were you given a lot of love as a child?' therapy, more like the 'I have got to get this off my chest', 'why is that bloke indicating round that bend at 18mph?' type of therapy.

The optimistic business ideas, bizarre invention ideas and constant random thoughts late at night will continue. So will the outward-bound missions, the after-school clubs and the daily madness at home.

And hopefully so will the football - after all, isn't it every boy's dream?